Trevor Watt

Union Theol Sem
New York,
Sept 1958

LB bookshed
408
Nov. 27

Christianity AND
THE *Existentialists*

Christianity AND THE *Existentialists*.

EDITED BY

CARL MICHALSON

CHARLES SCRIBNER'S SONS NEW YORK

B
819
.M5
(3)

There is no description so hard,

nor assuredly so profitable,

as is the description of a man's own self.

MONTAIGNE

CONTENTS

ILLUSTRATIONS

PREFACE

The chapters included in this volume were delivered in their original form as public lectures in Craig Chapel of Drew University during the academic year 1953–54. They comprise the fifteenth series of lectures in Christian Biography on a foundation established by President and Mrs. Ezra Squier Tipple.

The selection of the participants in the lectureship followed easily upon the choice of the subject. The lecturers were assembled under a commission entitled "The Challenge of Christian Existentialism." The major motive in this title is clear. A cultural movement which is exercising so great an influence upon the reformulation of Christian thought deserves to be appraised. But how does one decide which among existentialists past and present can be embraced within the limits of a lectureship on "*Christian* biography"?

Here a certain arbitrariness entered in, dictated partly by a lack of unanimity about whether there can be a "Christian" existentialism, partly by the spatial limits of the project. Avowed atheists like Nietzsche, Jean-Paul Sartre, Albert Camus, and Simone de Beauvoir are not included. But, then, neither are the avowed theists, Martin Buber and Karl Jaspers. It could be observed that Buber and Jaspers, while theists, are not within the Christian Church. But Fyodor Dostoevsky, Max Scheler, and Emmanuel Mounier professed Christianity, and they are not included.

It would be the consensus of the authors of this volume that any one of these existentialists could have been included in this study with profit to the Christian understanding. The presence of Martin Heidegger in the series, although he is customarily lumped with the atheistic existentialists, is proof of that, as is Paul Tillich's use of the most turbulent forms of modern art.

The selection, then, has been based not so much on the knowledge that these certain existentialists were also Christians, but rather on the special pertinence these particular men and movements have for Christianity today. What this pertinence is will, of course, be the burden of the several chapters.

C. M.

DREW FOREST
MADISON, N. J.

Christianity AND
THE *Existentialists*

1. *What Is Existentialism?*

"Existentialism" is one of the magic words of our time. When the word is used it seems capable of powers all out of proportion to its size. It can enchant with curiosity and a passionate eagerness to know. Or it can cast a spell of hostility and sometimes even a repressive anxiety to put it out of mind. Utter the word "existentialism" in a crowd and some will gather to learn, others will run for shelter. Ask a man if he is an existentialist, and if he does not show embarrassment, he may act annoyed, as if the answer would tend to incriminate. Ask a man— who in other respects seems quite at home in his world —ask him what existentialism is, and you may just as well have caught him peeking through a keyhole. That is why one may say existentialism is a magic word. Use it,

and you cannot always account for the consequences.
It may transform a scullery maid into a princess. It may
as easily graft a sausage to your nose.

At least there are very few among the literate people
of the world who by now have not so much as heard
whether there be an existentialism. Its influence ranges
all the way from styles in hats to the most serious technical philosophies. One may know of it chiefly from the
cabarets he has visited, or one may know of it from his
tilts with learned journals. But there is a common de-
nominator in the information. The suspicion is that
somehow existentialism is a clandestine wedding of
nordic melancholy with Parisian pornography.

This suspicion strikes close to the truth. Fortunately,
therefore, the road to an understanding of existentialism
need not by-pass what people at large suspect about it.
For instance, there *is* in existentialism a shocking sen-
sualism, an erotic realism, a tearful and throbbing meeting of skin against skin which, so characteristically
French, appreciates propinquity of heart and finger-tip.
There *are* in existentialism passionate nocturnal dialogues
in which two isolated souls join together their "I" and
"Thou" with burden of meaning which only confessions
of faith can carry—glances and words that break open
doors in tightly locked lives and give them the rightful
consolation of companionship, the nearly holy communion of incorporation.

At the same time, there is in existentialism a sentiment of constantly living over cracking earth, or at the
foot of live volcanoes, or in a land where people fight
two wars in every lifetime. Some cannot face their insecurity continually without developing a heightened
consciousness of themselves. A protracted sense of panic,
a variegated spectrum of inner moods draws one's atten-

tion deep into himself. There he interrogates himself
for his identity and then goes out again to ask whatever
powers there be what hope there is for him. A brooding
spirit is the seed-bed of apocalypticism. And yet, a radically examined melancholy will entertain no hopes that
violate the promise which one tastes when he meets his
spirit at its deepest levels.

Here, then, is the initial question. Can these popular
and essentially true but vague presentiments about existentialism be drawn into any kind of pattern? Can this
preliminary pattern be augmented in a manner to en-
hance one's maturing contacts with the subject? In short,
can existentialism be defined?

THE HAZARDS OF DEFINITION

The answer to that question is "yes" and "no." One
hesitates to refuse a definition for fear he would be
judged incompetent. One hesitates to consent to one
because of the enormous gap between definition and
existence. Definitions are concepts which, if they are
well made, speed directly to your brain. As such, they
are very efficient, especially if one is dealing at a logical
or a technological level. But the problem of defining
existentialism is like the problem of defining a flavor or
an odor. What is defined moves in a different medium
from the definition.

"Existentialism is a way of life which involves one's total self in
an attitude of complete seriousness about himself."

That is a fair preliminary definition, but it is aimed at
your head alone. Hence, the definiton of a process involving your total self actually lodges in your brain without involving more than a very small part of yourself.

You are existing when you are self-consciously immersed in living, not merely when you are thinking about living.

For this reason, many of the existentialists prefer the medium of poetry, drama, and the novel to the prosaic, conceptual medium of philosophy. Kierkegaard wrote in the style he called "indirect communication," which is his way of saying that he avoided propositions contrived to inform. It was rather his mission to write in such a way as to make his readers exist, to put them through experiences which his readers—in most cases professors, preachers, and students—would much prefer to define, memorize, and thereby terminate. Heidegger originally chose a method of direct discourse but kept it so thick that while it seemed aimed at the head, there were few heads permeable enough to absorb it. And now after years of silence, which is a philosophically reputable alternative to speech, Heidegger has taken to a medium second only to poetry in suitability, namely, the praise of poetry. It is his method of talking about reality without blocking the path between reality itself and living men. Marcel and Sartre have chosen drama, the novel, and even music. And Berdyaev, while he persists in defining after the method of the academic philosophies, continually reminds his readers that he knows definitions are not the thing.

Existentialism, you see, involves more what you do than what you think. Therefore definitions of existentialism would betray its very nature by encouraging only thought where action is required. This is why many traditionally oriented philosophers cannot accept existentialism as a serious philosophy. It resists the systematic and analytical operations usually associated with the philosophical enterprise.

At the same time, thinking is significantly related to

doing. Is it not quite possible to define your cake and eat it too? And is there not a savory reciprocity between the two acts? Likewise, it would seem that definitions or systematic language, if they maintained loyalty to the levels of existence which are avowedly deeper and more authentic than concept and language, would be a valuable index to what is really the meaning of existence and a valuable guide to one's proper engagement with reality. You are existing when you are seriously immersed in living, and you are thinking existentially when you are bringing your thoughts into captivity to the concerned pursuit of the authentic life.

It is this kind of reciprocity between existence and thoughts about existence which has brought existentialism from the turbulent and meaningful silence of existence into articulation as a philosophy. Hereafter, a philosophy which does not deliberately retain in its method the distinction between reality as engaged by one's whole life and reality as thought, between attitude toward reality and content about reality cannot be regarded as an existential *philosophy*. There is an existential way of living and there is an existential method of interpreting life. The two are reciprocally related, hence, to be neither confused nor separated. Just last week I advised a student that a certain issue he was facing could probably be resolved by a decision. He responded to the effect that he had often heard these words, "resolution" and "decision," and had even jotted them down, meaning to look into them some day. Well, one who thinks in a castle and lives in a dog house is not existing for he has not immersed himself in either. One who murmurs in his beer, "I wish I were dead," would only really be existing if he were at that moment quaffing poison.

EXISTENTIALISM AS SERIOUS PHILOSOPHY

As soon as one asks the question about what existentialism is, one enters the realm of existential philosophy. That means one ought to be prepared to pay the price that comes with philosophical reflection, to enter into the philosophical situation and to abide by the rules of the craft.

Now the thing that makes a philosophy significant is the very thing that makes it difficult. It is true that every philosopher desires to be in continuity with the whole family of philosophy as far back as the genealogy can be traced. Novelty and philosophy are alien concepts in that sense, and there is a great family loyalty among philosophers. Consequently, no existential philosopher is happy seeing existentialism paraded as a fad.

At the same time, it is just as true that no philosopher is completely contented with the progress of philosophy to this date. Major predicaments which philosophers assume as their profound burden still remain unresolved. The constant aspiration of philosophers is to overcome the limitations which have kept others from untying the stubbornest knots in reality. The sign of a major philosophy is its ability to place a question-mark against any previous philosophy by the revolutionary character of its own method. Aristotle did it to Plato, and Descartes and Bacon did it to Aristotle. Kant did it to Descartes, and Hegel did it to Kant. The philosophical method of Hegel has since been gnawed away by a host of materialisms, pragmatisms, positivisms and neo-idealisms, but philosophy at the present moment is in the ambiguous position of having discredited its last great methodologist without successfully supplanting him. Is it *now* true that no philosopher can touch existentialism without radical shock to his system? And has existentialism a sufficient stature to assume the kind of burden which the great philosophies of the past have carried? These are the questions being asked about existentialism today. Whatever the answers, the questions label it as a serious and significant contemporary philosophy.

This very significance of existentialism, however, makes it so difficult to understand. If it is a serious philosophy, it is tied to the philosophical past, so that from that standpoint, if you know a little about the history of philosophy, you should find it easy to appropriate existentialism. But if it is a significant philosophy, it is oriented to the future, as well. It is pioneering and revolutionary. It is *avant garde.* Hence, notwithstanding your previous fraternal ties with philosophy, your participation in existentialism will require some initiation.

Because this is quite formally the case, throughout the reading of this book some will comment, "ridiculous," and others, "everybody knows that." And by these statements the reader will classify himself. For, as the German philosopher, Husserl, has indicated, there are several stages in the appropriation of a *new* philosophical viewpoint. The *second* stage is the feeling of its redundancy. For either the philosophy has made its way around to the extent that its jargon is now somewhat familiar to you, or it is so basically illuminating when you hear it that you cannot believe Plato was not bright enough to have thought of it first.

For most, however, existentialism is in the *first* stage. They will feel its absurdity. But that would be expected of a philosophy which in some important way has gone beyond the past and anything you yourself would therefore be expected to know. The Spanish philosopher, Ortega y Gasset, has said of Heidegger that his use of words reminds one of a pearl diver who goes down very deep to bring up hidden pearls between his teeth, but it may be questioned whether Heidegger ever comes back up. A philosopher's language, that is, is required to be deep, but ought it not also be clear; it goes down, but ought it not come back to the surface? Ortega defends Heidegger on the grounds that he is not an author but a thinker. The thinker is not expected to be clear and distinct. That is the vocation of the author. The problem of the thinker is that he must discover what no one else knows and yet he is expected to render it in a language which antedates his discovery. Hegel felt this wretched problem, as you must have felt it if you have read Hegel. The unintelligibility of philosophy, he complained, is due not so much to one's incapacity for abstract thinking as to one's unwillingness to move beyond the use of familiar ideas. "One consequence of this weakness," he has said, "is that authors, preachers, and orators are found most intelligible, when they speak of things which their readers or hearers already know by rote,—things which the latter are conversant with, and which require no explanation." [1] * But "the thinker," says Ortega, "has no other way out than to create a language in order to make himself understood. He cannot use the language which is common to all." [2] Were he to do so, he would commit what A. N. Whitehead calls the "fallacy of the perfect dictionary." Refusing to do so, he must introduce a courageous kind of terminological clarity transcending the philosophical limits of ordinary speech. One soon discovers, then, that he

* The notes, referring chiefly to sources, will be found at the back of the book.

must learn to talk all over again. He must learn to talk philosophically before he can think philosophically.

Resistance to existentialism is not limited to these purely semantic and syntactical matters, however. For *muteness* is closely related to deafness. One must keep his ear to the ground before he can talk existentially, and that kind of basic living is the hardest of all to come by. What do you suppose Unamuno had in mind when he said, "If one of Ibsen's dramas should please the audience in one of our theatres, I would begin to doubt its worth"? He simply meant that no one enjoys having the mask lifted from his face or conventional securities pulled away from him. No one finds pleasure in the feeling that the meaning of life is somehow contingent upon a radical cross-examination of oneself and on an absolute involvement in what is there revealed. No one relishes the prospect that the very status of being is at stake in him. Nor is the outlook of profound personal suffering a very considerable incentive. Yet, existentialism holds out no less than this. To be existentially vocal requires one to be an auditor of existence at these deepest levels.

Socrates was one of the first existential philosophers. By his interrogation he could reduce the citizens to a humiliating consciousness of their ignorance, a humiliation only slightly abated by his own admission of ignorance. In another sense, however, existentialism dates back only as far as the Apostle Paul, for whom not intellectual doubt with its threat of meaninglessness, but guilt and death were the realities that menaced man. One does not truly exist until one knows himself, as the oracle at Delphi advised Socrates. But does one know himself until he has been faced not simply with his ig-

norance but with his death and with his moral burden
as well? Western philosophy, beginning as it does in
Socrates and his several predecessors, begins likewise in
wonder, that fundamentally honest, Socratic, intellectual
curiosity which Descartes later labelled doubt. But
philosophy in the existentialist view begins in despair,
the despair of an existence faced by a predicament which
it can only survive either through impudent self-will or
through the hope of rescue from beyond oneself. Such
psychologically oppressive phenomena as guilt and death
induce in man the interior agony so commonly denoted
in our day by anxiety. One can presumably make his
peace with his ignorance, especially when the ignorance
is of matters which are not particularly crucial to one's
on-going life. You can be just without defining justice
and you can be a friend without defining friendship. But
can you be a man in any fundamental sense without
penetrating the meaning of your guilt and death? Well,
existentialism is based upon the supposition that to exist
is to face up to the conditions of life which generate
these anxieties about our very being.

WHAT IT MEANS "TO EXIST"

A galaxy of meanings clusters around the word "existence" giving the philosophy its distinctiveness. Existence is not a thing with predicates. The verb "to be" in
the existential syntax is not a copula which binds a string
of attributes to some substance. One does not say of man,
he *Is,* and then go on to add a predicate object, such as,
he is "a thinking thing." One simply says, he is. Man *is*
his existence. There is nothing more specific one can
say. *To exist is what a man is.*

But then one must not rewrite Shakespeare as the

Scholastic philosopher does and say of a man, "To be—
that is the answer." Existence is not the be all and end
all for man. For facing the limits in what man takes to
be his existence, he can only realize that being itself is
under question because of the threats to his being which
are productive of his anxious mood. "To be or not to
be—that is the *question*." The glory and the curse of
man is his ability to sense his possible *non*-being. *To
exist is to realize man can be nothing.*

The clues to that discovery, however, lie in the subjective moods of man—his fears and dread, his cares
and sense of guilt. Existentialism is the first serious
philosophy in the entire history of philosophy to place
such trust in subjective moods. From the days of Socrates to the present, a mood has been classified as
opinion and hence least likely to contribute to sound
judgment. Moods have been traditionally traced back to
weaknesses in man which life in the body forces upon
him. A rational man, it is thought, would rise above his
moods. But the existential man immerses himself in his
moods to find within them a trustworthy index to reality.
These moods are not the accidental product of his ner-
vous system but a revelatory reading in his existence. As
he buffets the containing wall of reality he can gauge
the pattern which describes himself. These moods are
the sentient antennae which feel out the boundaries
marking the area within which one's life may be well
led, the radar devices of the spirit which engage not
simply the enemies and obstructions on the way to man's
authentic selfhood, but the positive conditions of reality
as well. *To exist is to take seriously these messages from
deep within oneself.*

This stress on subjectivity is of a piece with existential
individualism. One cannot know himself by applying to

his life the universally valid truths which come from mathematical and syllogistic reasoning. Take the proposition, "All men are mortal." This is a philosophical generalization which it has rarely occurred to anyone to contest. But it has contributed about as much to man's understanding of himself as Plato's definition of man as a "featherless bi-ped." When one faces, however, the matter of his own possible non-being and says, "Death is *for me*," then philosophical insight merges with existential concern.

Some truths are not really true until they are related to an existing individual. There is the little boy Josiah Royce tells about, who would not replace his broken lead soldier with another, even though it was cast from an identical mold. Was he simply stubborn? Not at all. He was a junior existentialist. The individual was more real than the universal. Quite clearly this is not the individualism of which Kant and the eighteenth century knew, which saw in every man the essence of manhood in general and from that inferred that the rights of all individuals are the same. It is rather the individualism of the nineteenth century—of Goethe, Stirner, and Nietzsche—which saw in each man a singular life, unrepeatable in anyone else, untransferable to anyone else. One can only infer from this individualism that the rights of each individual are unique. It was this individualism to which Kierkegaard referred when he announced, "My category is the individual." It is this individualism which Heidegger and Jaspers attest when they realize no man can die another man's death for him. There is no general mold from which all men are cast. If there were, a man could know himself from his arm chair or his ivory tower: by reflection on the rational pattern of manhood in general. Because there is no such pattern, a man may know himself only by living his own life seriously and reflecting upon it. *To exist is to be unique.*

It is a popular mistake to conclude from existential individualism that it has no capacity for social life. It is only true that social relations are not here based upon an eighteenth-century view of the individual which lumps him gregariously with the whole herd of man. Social relations which are based upon existential individualism will be initiated in the creative force of personal volition. Which means when individuals come together, they will not lose their identity by social proximity. Their social resoluteness paradoxically intensifies their individuality. At the same time, their individuality will not jeopardize sociality, for their link with their fellow-man will not be based upon the tepid and irresolute assumption that birds of a feather flock together. It will be based upon the responsible resoluteness of an inter-personal fidelity.

To exist, in fact, precisely means to reach beyond one's own being. To exist means to stand outside oneself, to extend beyond oneself. When a seriously existing man allows his life to undergo interrogation to its very roots, he will sense that his life is bottomless. He will not find himself by referring simply to himself. As Kierkegaard has said, it is as if he had been shipwrecked, and at a point on the sea where 70,000 fathoms of water were his sole support. A man thrown into the sea can only thrash about. He may discover by his very thrashing that he supports himself. Atheistic existentialism inclines to that opinion. Or his thrashing arms may hit upon some more substantial hope outside himself. Metaphysical and theistic existentialism follows this suggestion.

The danger seen in the existential individualism, therefore, is not so much the danger that one will remain locked up in isolation from society, *cor incurvatum in se,* a heart curled up within itself. Man's dominant passions are social and centrifugal. The panic of the inner life urges one to move beyond himself to alliances that provide stability which he does not find within him. The danger is rather that the individual, whose passion it is to reach out, will attach himself to inauthentic objects, objects which cannot and ought not support him. Religiously viewed, this would be idolatry. Psychologically viewed, it would be a diseased kind of emotional dependence. Socially viewed, it would be a parasitical kind of welfare-ism.

For these reasons, existentialism always appears in the extremes either of philosophical nihilism, as in Sartre and Camus, or of philosophical faith, as in Marcel and Berdyaev. Either the existentialist resolves to go it alone, notwithstanding the craziness of it, which is nihilism, or he transcends himself in what Marcel likes to call a *sursum corda,* which is faith. The relations of the nihilist to others are based upon a courageous but fatiguing resolve which safeguards for others the independence one cherishes for oneself. Here a chronic individualist stoically sustains social loyalty. On the other hand, the relations of the fideist to others are subsumed under a comprehensive, all-embracing relation, a higher dependence, the normal expression of which is creative social interdependence, neither emotionally weak nor socially parasitical, because metaphysically grounded. In either case, however, *to exist is to be with and for another.*

Strictly speaking, then, existence is a term applicable only to man. The mineral, vegetable, and animal worlds, whatever their level of evolution, or their capacity to perceive relations, do not reach out with the same vol-

untary passion as a man does, though existentialism is
much closer in its view to biology than to mathematics.
And the anxiety which a calculating complex of stimuli
and responses can induce in an animal is scarcely com-
parable to the agitation that follows when one con-
templates himself in his agitation, as a man can and as
an animal apparently cannot. One need only read the
sarcastic treatment of Pavlovism in the novels of Arthur
Koestler to sense that distinction. As for God, he does
not exist. God and animals have that in common. Neither
transcends itself. The animal cannot, due to the blind-
ness of his instincts. God need not, due to the absence
of anything beyond him to require his reach. Man alone
is the highly specialized kind of reality called existence.
Existentialism for that reason is sometimes referred to as
a humanism (Sartre) or a personalism (Mounier and
Berdyaev). *To exist is to be human.*

Because existentialism makes man central to its method, it has also often been called a philosophical anthropology. Some existentialists accept the label: Berdyaev,
for instance, for whom, as for Feuerbach before him,
philosophy *is* anthropology. Can one who is not a god
start higher than with man? But in Berdyaev as in
Kierkegaard and Marcel, the study of man is filled with
escalator operations. It reveals a *tour de force* in the
structure of reality, a directional urge which the philosopher does not create but finds. The study of man may
lead one to the first principles of metaphysics or even
to the God of religion, but at least to sources of authenticity beyond man himself. In Jaspers, for instance, the
interpretation of existence is the doorway to a very reverent kind of metaphysics. The serious experiences of man
are taken to be symbols of the hidden reality which
man's life presupposes. In Sartre and Heidegger, more-

over, the existential investigation of man is neither simply anthropology nor theology and metaphysics. It is
what is called "fundamental ontology," a study of the
very structure of being, wherever it is found, from the
standpoint of the way being appears in the human
existence. *To exist is to reveal the character of being
itself.*

The biggest gap between existentialism and other current philosophies lies in its unwillingness to be bound by
the standards of the sciences. Kierkegaard repudiated
the scientific pretension in Hegel's system. In their
philosophies of life, Nietzsche and Dilthey saw that
man's life is history and not nature. While nature can be
objectified and rationalized, history is too ambiguous to
be grasped. It can only be lived through and reflected
upon. The primary data for the life philosophies are
therefore found in confessions and memoirs, private
journals and autobiography, and these are considered
more valuable philosophically than the tests and meas-
ures closer to the exact sciences. The natural sciences are
fine implements for assessing the realm of objects and
problems, the realm of things man holds. But how shall
they interpret the realm which holds man, the ontological
subtleties in a man's struggle for his very being? Scientific philosophies recognize their own methodological
limits in relation to the mysteries normally dealt with by
metaphysicians. But some of them manifest a dog-in-the-
manger mentality. They deny to other methods the
philosophical right to pursue meanings inaccessible to
their own. What would become of the pursuit of wisdom
in philosophy today if all philosophy were to capitulate
to the dogma of logical positivism? Is every question a
meaningless question if it cannot be given a perceptually
demonstrable answer? Yet existentialism and logical pos-

itivism are the ranking philosophies of the day (with the possible exception of process philosophy). Against this growing tendency in the philosophy of the schools to dismiss as meaningless all reference to the perplexities which simply matter most to men, existentialism has been asserting the essential philosophical significance of such attitudes as anxiety and guilt, devotion and surrender, confession and prophecy, mystery and salvation. It will not risk the pathetic blunder of the scientist in Hawthorne's story, who removed the birthmark from his wife's face "only to discover it was the bond by which an angelic spirit kept itself in union with a mortal frame." *To exist is to value personal authenticity more highly than scientific exactitude.*

BIOGRAPHY AND EXISTENTIALISM

The kinship between existentialism and biography, then, should be quite apparent. Existentialism is a method of interpreting life which is based upon an attitude of seriousness in living. The biography of an existentialist satisfies more than one's curiosity about a significant life. Ever since Plutarch, biography has been the art of getting inside the letters and memoirs, the dreams and confessions of individuals, not simply to outline their thoughts or to chronicle their deeds but to fathom their spirits. "My design," said Plutarch, "is not to write histories, but lives." Thereupon, he simply gave an account of individual men as they existed.

There is a suspicion, however, that Plutarch selected his "lives" in terms of pre-established human types, consonant with his own brand of idealism, the result being that his "lives" were considered as "typical." To assemble a group of biographies together under a single title,

"The Existentialists," would seem to be transparent
Plutarchianism and a manifest violation of the existential claim to the uniqueness of the individual. A reading
of these biographies will easily dispel that fear, however.
For there is an existential way of writing biography and
an existential way of reading biography.

The patent truth about existential biography is not
simply that the life is a-typical, which is to say unique,
though that is true. For instance, one can never learn to
exist by imitating Kierkegaard. He will only end by
breaking up his romance, being ashamed of his father,
and dying at age forty-two. One could learn, however,
by participating deeply in Kierkegaard's spirit to face
seriously one's own loves, one's own sense of guilt, and
one's own incomparable death. That, then, is the more
apparent truth in existential biography. When it is read,
it should give one the sense of one's own unique existence. But then the task of existential biography, it would
seem, would be so to present the lives of others as best
to reveal to oneself his own life. This would require—to
adopt a metaphor from Kierkegaard—that the biography assume the properties of a nettle which, when you
touch it, makes you aware more of yourself than of the
nettle. When the life of a great man is existentially com-
municated it will simultaneously repel the auditor from
grasping the subject matter and provide an entre into
the subject that matters most, which is oneself.

Almost every one of the existentialists to be considered in these biographies has obligingly written his
philosophy at some time or other in the form of autobiography, or journal. But the subject-matter of these
journals could well disappoint the unsuspecting reader.
Kierkegaard, for instance, is surely autobiographical in
his *Diary of a Seducer,* but whatever bedroom scenes one

comes upon there are philosophical outcries of a soul wrestling in his dreams with angels. Nor will one find in these succeeding chapters any detailed gossip about the daily affairs in the lives of the existentialists. He will rather find confessions of the inner life which, when heard, should give the reader access to the echoing chambers of his own inner life.

EXISTENTIALISM AND CHRISTIANITY

What of the relation of existentialism to Christianity? As you know, existential philosophers today range all the way from the most insolent atheists to the most devout Christians, from a left-bank nihilist like Sartre to such pious Catholics as Marcel, a convert to Rome, and Berdyaev, an Eastern Orthodox Christian. And, as Berdyaev has said, "When a philosopher is a believing Christian, it is quite inconceivable that his philosophy should remain unaffected by his religious convictions."

Possibly you have noticed that for this book the most sanitary of the existentialists have been selected. Even so, there is some difference of opinion—as will be manifested among these very chapters—as to the Christian significance of even the most nearly Christian existentialists. Some interpreters find existentialism close to Christianity and refer to it as "a secularized Paulinism" or "Theresa and John of the Cross secularized into an anthropological myth." Among these, however, some reject it in order to remain with the original Biblical or mystical theology (Thielicke, Przywara), while others reject the Christian source and live by the derivative (Kamlah). Still others, referring to existentialism as a "secular, philosophical presentation of the New Testament view of human existence," accept it as a guide to

the modern Christian man's understanding of himself
(Bultmann and his followers).

One can refer to the apparent relation between Christianity and existentialism indifferently, as Karl Barth
has done in his little writing on Bultmann's thought:
"In all theological soup today there float some philosophical fragments." [3] Or one can become violent about
it, as Nietzsche did when he charged that the Protestant
pastor is the father of German philosophy, and deplored
the cunning theology at the base of German philosophy.

Irrespective of what one may believe to be the relation
between any philosophy and the Christian faith, it is an
intellectual fact that existential philosophy is now exert-
ing a telling influence upon the elucidation of the Christian faith. It becomes the obligation of the interpreter
to trace the lines along which the interaction between
existentialism and Christianity is taking place and to
evaluate its significance.

Anyone who understands the poignant sense of human
need in existentialism could concede that existentialism
is at least a road to Bethlehem, or better, to Calvary.
Candid self-understanding leads one to hopes that lie
beyond oneself. But at the end of that road one may as
easily find only a manger of straw as find the Messiah.
One may as easily find only two thieves as find the suffering savior. The theological relevance of such a philosophical road will depend largely upon what one expects
of a philosophy. Is it autonomous, so that it can resolve
all life's mysteries without the aid of a faith? Has it a
pre-established harmony with some particular faith, so
that it may unfailingly lead one to that faith? Or does it
exercise the sort of obstetric force upon life which de-
livers one's faith into understanding without in any way
claiming paternity to that faith?

In some ways there are only two living religions of the world today—Christianity and communism; and existentialism is more often classified with communism than with Christianity, on the grounds that it is anti-religious. To be sure, both communism and existentialism are usually atheistic and anti-clerical. But the difference between them is instructive. Communism, notwithstanding its doctrinaire atheism, has been able to deify mammon and the purveyors of mammon. Existentialism will not settle for half-gods. Communism, notwithstanding its aggressive anti-clericalism, has been able to erect a clericalism of its own in an elaborate hierarchical system of authorities. Existentialism will let nothing come between a man and his highest authority. A philosophy which makes plausible substitutes for Christian realities is, indeed, as much a menace to Christianity as is idolatry in any form. A philosophy which puts nothing in the place of God may legitimately be called atheistic, but it can never be called idolatrous. Communism puts false gods in the place of the God of the Christian faith. This turns its atheism into a substitute faith. Existentialism does not put Jesus in the manger or Christ on the middle cross, but it will put nothing else there, either. This is its Christian advantage over such religious philosophies as Stoicism which with its pious language and self-sufficient world-view in almost every detail rendered the Christian faith superfluous. This question, then, must be faced: If a philosophy can ever do anything to prepare the way for the Christ in our culture today, will it not be the very philosophy which refuses to supplant him? Existentialism nurses an aching void, keeps the wounds of man open until an authentically healing agent can be applied. Existentialism sponsors what the poet Hölderlin called "a holy emptiness" which turns its atheism into a wistful stretching out for reality, a noumenal hunger, a movement of the spirit which keeps a sensitive openness upward toward the God who must reveal Himself if He is to be known.

What some reject as straw in existentialism may yet turn out to be a sound philosophical yearning, a yearning for a redemption to which no philosophy is either virginal or divine enough to give birth. Can the language of philosophy ever mount higher—*ought* it ever, *need* it ever mount higher than the existential passion in the porous verse of the young Nietzsche,

> "I want to know you, Unknown One,
> You who are reaching deep into my soul
> And ravaging my life, a savage gale.
> You inconceivable yet related one!
> I want to know you—even serve." [4]

H. RICHARD NIEBUHR

2. *Sören Kierkegaard*

One is tempted to speak of Sören Kierkegaard in the
paradoxes that he loved; to say, for instance, that while
he was born in 1813 and died in 1855, "Christianly
speaking" he began to die in 1813 and to live in 1855;
that he was a more than double-minded man, who
played many parts and lost himself in them, while all
the time pursuing one aim; that he was a mystifier who
brought clarity into our human confusion; that he was
one of the most violently anti-religious writers of the
nineteenth century and one of its devoutest Christians.
Such paradoxes can be multiplied almost without limit:
they indicate how difficult it is to know and to interpret
this strange man.

THE INTRUSIVE STRANGER

There are a number of ways in which we can try to assuage the confusion into which a meeting with Kierkegaard throws us. One way that commends itself to our time is, of course, the attempt to analyze psychologically this evidently abnormal character: as abnormal as Nietzsche and Van Gogh. The melancholy that marked him and to which he gave frequent expression despite his efforts to dissemble it; the strange relation to a father whose soul was heavy with the sense of guilt; the involved and painful story of his love for Regina Olsen and of the broken engagement; the almost semi-Messianic ideas that come to appearance toward the end of his career; the challenge he issued to *The Corsair* to make him the butt of ridicule; these and other data indicate the presence of a sick mind. So a self-confident healthy-mindedness undertakes to dismiss him as another genius at the edge of madness. But then the question arises for healthy-mindedness as to where the genius stops and where the madness begins. And once this doubt has entered another doubt arises, whether indeed this healthy-mindedness is as healthy as it thinks it is or as sick as Kierkegaard's diagnosis of it indicates. Is not this feeling of soundness perhaps hallucination, a symptom of the sickness unto death? Is this optimism a flight from reality, this extroverted objectivism a determined effort to escape from self-knowledge through distraction? Does not "healthy-mindedness" depend for its continuance on the construction of an illusory world, in which the self affirms its security though it knows what it cannot acknowledge to be true: that existence is infinitely precarious?

We may attempt in another way to rid ourselves of the intrusive stranger who causes us so much perplexity. We may put him into his proper place in history, explaining him as a product of his times and so consigning him to the dead past. He is one of those young Hegelians who in devotion to their master's method set up antitheses to the thesis Hegel proposed. Kierkegaard is the protester, the reactive thinker, who can be understood against the background of what he reacted against. He reacted against the systematic thesis of Hegelianism with the antithesis of non-systematic thought; against the thesis that everything leads to synthesis with the antithesis that everything leads to antithesis; against the thesis that the idea objectifies itself with the antithesis that it subjectifies itself, etc. Having put him into the historical context we may then hang his portrait on the wall with our pictures of other thinkers of the past, members of the great chain of witnesses to truth who made their contributions and passed on. But Kierkegaard resists our efforts to dispose of him in this fashion. For one thing he belongs less to the history of nineteenth century thought than to that of the twentieth. He destroys, not only by his explicit reflections but by the example his own career affords, this notion about history that it is past. He makes himself contemporaneous with us. And he does not so much lead us to think about the systems of his time and the necessity of protests against them as about our systems and about our need to protest now. He calls attention not so much to the theses and antitheses, the polarities and ambivalences in his own existence as in ours. He will not keep his place in history; or, otherwise, he will not let us order our history into a nicely arranged series of events that have passed never to be resurrected.

There is a third way of reducing this strange phenomenon to order so that we can forget him and go on with our business. We can classify him; having put him into his proper category we shall then know what attitude to take toward him. He is an existentialist philosopher who like the other existentialist philosophers, such as Jaspers and Heidegger, is interested in the problem of being and takes personal existence as the clue to being, just as idealists take thought with idea, empiricists experience with its sense data, and vitalists life, as the clues to reality. Is not the existentialist philosopher one who calls attention to the importance of answering the question, What am I? as a way of learning to answer, What does "to be" mean? But then Kierkegaard confounds us again by his complete lack of interest in the question of what being is, and by his insistence that the ethical question not only takes precedence over the metaphysical but can ethically never be abandoned in favor of the latter. The question is not what being is, but how I can become myself.

However we seek to dispose of him, by means of any of the familiar devices that enable us to reduce living men to ideas or objects towards which we can take our preconditioned attitudes, Kierkegaard returns, a perplexing and disquieting person. He remains the individual, subjective self who will not allow himself to be classified or objectivised. And he remains an elusive figure, who is forever directing our attention away from himself to ourselves.

This is a peculiar phenomenon in human history—a thinker who is always this individual thinking and who can never be reduced to his thought; a thinker who is always at the same time pointing away from himself to us so that when we think with him we think about ourselves. The phenomenon is not wholly peculiar, for Kierkegaard is very much like his great hero Socrates, whose wisdom consisted in the knowledge of his ignorance, whose imperative was 'know thyself,' whose philosophy of life was reduplicated in his living and his dying, who was a comic and a tragic figure, who was the father of philosophers but the father of no philosophy. Socrates is also always an individual thinking rather than a set of ideas; he always excites those who listen to him to reflect upon their own thought and to discover their own ignorance. Both of these men are philosophical Nathans who by means of stories and questions lead us to the critical juncture where we hear the disturbing adjuration, "Thou art the man." Yet Kierkegaard is a Christian Socrates. His individual reflection leads less to the individual's discovery of his ignorance than of guilt and the utter contingency of being; he exists less in knowledge and more in faith; his *daimon* is Jesus Christ; the comic and tragic in his life appear in Christian perspectives, as the comic disproportion between the disciple and the Master he undertakes to imitate, and as his tragic participation in the cross.

Such men as these cannot be talked about without falsifying them. There is something comic about the pretentiousness of the academic lecturer who undertakes to speak for an hour about the Socratic method of eliciting knowledge through questioning. It is comic also to be very wise about Socrates' knowledge of his ignorance. It is even more ridiculous when one speaks directly about Kierkegaard—this man whose genius lies in his indirection and whose concern it is that we should be concerned with ourselves. When we speak about him directly it is as though we were following a series of signs on the road, which read "This way to the sign-post," knowing all the while that when we arrive at the sign-post we will find a hand pointing nowhere except directly at us.

Nevertheless we shall make this ridiculous venture along with many who have gone before, accepting the predicament of the teacher who can teach nothing but only point his hearers to the place where they may learn.

"THE MONSTROUS ILLUSION"

Among those who have talked about Kierkegaard as well as with him is Sören Kierkegaard himself. In 1848 after the period of intense productivity out of which had come *Either-Or, The Stages on Life's Way, The Philosophical Fragments, The Concluding Unscientific Postscript* and many *Edifying Discourses,* he wrote but did not publish a little work entitled *The Point of View for My Work as an Author—A Report to History.* It was a kind of *Apologia Pro Vita Sua* in which he defended himself against misunderstanding. He did not publish the book because it was a report to history by one who predicted that "some day not only my writings but my whole life, all the intriguing mystery of the machine, will be studied and studied." But there may have been another reason; he may have discerned something wrong, something off-key, in this effort to "bear witness to himself" and so to direct attention away from that to which he witnessed. In *The Point of View* he wrote: ". . . the whole of my work as an author is related to Christianity, to the problem 'of becoming a Christian,' with direct or indirect polemic against the monstrous illusion we call Christendom, or against the illusion that in such a land as ours all are Christians. . . ." [1] This is a fair description of the duality of his work. It is on the one hand a sustained, subtle and vigorous attack on illusion, and particularly on Christian illusion. It is, on the other hand, a consistent effort to edify, to build up, to help individuals become Christians. And these two things belong together, not in a paradoxical or dialectical way, but as two sides of one shield.

The duality is partly represented in the two-fold nature of his literary production. On the one hand there are the aesthetic works, the essays and inventions of the professional writer; on the other hand there are the works of the preacher who had no authority to preach but could write *Edifying Discourses, Discourses for Communion on Friday* and *Christian Discourses*. The aesthetic works were published under pseudonymous authorship, being ascribed to such fictitious characters as Victor Eremita, Frater Taciturnus, Hilarious Bookbinder, Johannes Climacus and Anti-Climacus, but the discourses appeared under Kirkegaard's own name. The subtle reasons for this use of pseudonyms and of the Chinese puzzle methods Kierkegaard used in the aesthetic writings need not detain us here. But the fact that he used his own name in the publication of the edifying works evidently indicates that these represented his positive intention. In *The Point of View* he comments that a reader who "understands perfectly and appraises critically the individual aesthetic productions . . . will nevertheless totally misunderstand me, inasmuch as he does not understand the religious totality in my whole work as an author," while another reader who understands the works in "the totality of their religious reference, but does not understand a single one of the aesthetic productions contained in them—I would say that this lack of understanding is not an essential lack." [2] On the whole this duality of aesthetic and edifying works corresponds with the duality of the negative and positive tasks—the polemic against illusion and the effort to assist men to become Christians. On the whole this is true, but not completely; for the positive interest is present in aesthetic works, and there is much of the negative, that is, of the polemic against illusion, in the discourses.

1. *The Shadow World of Objects.* Kierkegaard's polemic against illusion does not begin directly with the fight against what he calls the "monstrous illusion of Christendom" but with an attack against something more general. He is profoundly aware, as all significant philosophers, religious teachers, scientists, painters, poets, dramatists have been, that "things are not what they seem." Each of them has understood that we human beings live in a world of shadows and that in our cave we tend to accept the shadows for reality. Each of them in his own way has sought to interpret the images for us and to put us into touch with the reality that is hidden by the appearance or revealed in it. One is tempted to divide them into two groups: those who call attention to the way in which appearance hides reality, and those who direct attention to the manner in which it reveals the real; the Platos and the Aristotles, the Augustines and the Thomases, the Tillichs and the Barths. Insofar as that division is useful we must put Kierkegaard in the former group. That "things are not what they seem" in his experience means that appearance hides reality. His whole work from one point of view can be regarded as an attack on the idea that appearance as such is any revelation of the reality of existence. Everything is a disguise, a seduction. And in this world of disguises the real man, intent on his real tasks, is not only disguised

but must disguise himself if he is to reveal anything. There is no other way.

2. *The Subject as Shadow.* Kierkegaard's attack upon illusion, however, is not simply this general polemic against the acceptance of appearance for reality. He is not only intent on communicating to others a general attitude of questioning and of scepticism toward appearances. He is more particularly concerned with certain specific illusions that arise out of the very conflict with illusion. As we human beings seek to penetrate through the seeming to the true we concentrate our attention on what is before us on the shadows that appear on the wall. We try to understand what we sense as pointers to what we cannot sense—to electrons and neutrons, to ideas and forms, to laws of nature and psychological complexes. We seek the reality behind the appearance by means of analysis, trying to discover the infinitely little, or by synthesis, trying to understand the infinitely great. But then there is always something we leave out of our reckoning and out of our description of the real, namely the self that is always compresent with its objects. Here we sit in the cave before the shadows on the rock and all our teachers as they seek to emancipate us from slavery to appearance try to direct our attention to the real *objects* that cast these shadows. And the more we attend to the objective the more we leave out of consideration the presence of ourselves and of our companions—these most real beings that can never become the *objects* of attention.

So a new illusion arises in consequence of our battle against illusions. The new illusion is that when we know the hidden objects, we know reality. But what of the subject that confronts these objects What about this self that has been left out? Kierkegaard is not an idealist who contends that objects before us are all projections of the private or universal subject and that we must therefore, if we would understand reality, turn to the study of the subject to see how he projects objects. That is not the point. The illusion does not consist in the belief that there is an objective world. It does not consist in the belief that the objective is real and that physics and metaphysics are ways to objective truth. Kierkegaard is well aware of the importance of these ways of knowing. The illusion consists rather in the belief that we, the selves in the cave, are like shadows of true objects, and that if we knew ourselves we would know something objective. It is the illusion which arises when having said, "In order to understand this objective reality I must be disinterested," I then conclude, "I am therefore essentially a disinterested man." I have failed to note that I could not be disinterested unless I were passionately interested in disinterestedness, that beyond and beneath this abstract knower there is the passionately concerned self. It is the illusion about reality which arises when I answer the question "Who am I?" by saying "I am a man" and then ascribe to myself the characteristics of objectively understood humanity and amidst all this fail to note that I am I and that what I esteem most about these human beings is not that they are men, but that each of them is potentially or actually an "I," a self, an individual subject, existing in all the inwardness, all the reflectiveness, all the tenuousness of selfhood. It is the illusion which appears when I define myself as rational being and thereupon substitute for the "I" the idea of reason, leaving out of account the individual self that not only reasons but sometimes believes against reason and is always passionately concerned. Idealism no less than realism in philosophy raises the new illusion, though the former "objectifies" the self more in the sense of making a thing out of it while the latter ignores it.

What we have left out in both instances in our concern for the objective is the immediate reality to himself or in himself of the individual subject. We have left out his existence as a feeling, sentient being, existing in the aesthetic sphere as one who pursues happiness; in the ethical as one who commits himself in decision; in the religious as the one who takes the risk of faith. We have left him out as "that individual" who is not a member of a species but the unique "I" in his here and now; we have left him out as the being who does not so much seek truth about the objective world as he exists in relations of truthfulness to himself and to others; we have left him out as the one who not only experiences feelings of love but binds himself by resolution to love, whether or not he will feel love; we have left him out in his poignant self-existence. We have left out of reality what cannot be known because it is behind every knowing. The illusion is that reality is something that can be known, when indeed it is something lived.

3. *Objective Christianity*. With this general attack on "objectivism" we can understand Kierkegaard's attack on the "monstrous illusion of Christendom." The monstrosity of the illusion comes to appearance in many forms. That something is wrong with Christianity has been known, of course, from the beginning of its career. And that this wrongness is connected with the disparity between appearance and reality has also been noted. Folk have looked at this historic appearance of Christianity and have said, "It is hypocritical. Look at the difference between its profession and its practice. It professes to follow one who gave up everything for the sake of men, who became poor that they might become rich.

But it is rich and seeks power." Or hypocrisy is discovered in the disagreement between the church's claims to holiness and catholicity and its existence in sin and conflict. "There is," says the reformer as well as the anti-Christian, "a duplicity in this Christianity. It seeks to present itself as something that it is not. Let it become inwardly what it pretends to be outwardly, or let it honestly present itself outwardly as what it is inwardly." A vast struggle goes on in the historic church, a great effort to make the appearance conform to the reality or the actual to the ideal and a great effort, also, to understand the reality behind the appearance.

Now, to be sure, Kierkegaard participates in this struggle directly and indirectly. He has a sharp eye—one of the sharpest—for duplicity. He sees the comedy and the tragedy present in our preaching, as we commend the meekness of our Lord Jesus Christ self-confidently and with a desire to increase the might of Christianity; as we speak proudly of that Christian humility which is so much more excellent than Aristotelean great-mindedness; as we proclaim anxiously the need for maintaining faith in God in order that we may not perish; or condemn as sinners those who do not believe in the doctrines of original sin or of the forgiveness of sins. How tragic it is, says Kierkegaard, that nobody laughs when the preacher reads in tones of great solemnity to an audience of the well-dressed, well-fed, well-taught, solid, leading citizens, assembled in the nobly built and richly ornamented church, the text from Paul's epistle: "Consider your call, brethren; not many of you were wise according to worldly standards, not many were powerful, not many were of noble birth; but God chose what is foolish in the world to shame the wise, God chose what is weak in the world to shame the strong, God chose what is low and despised in the world, even things that are not to bring to nothing things that are."

What is tragic here, however, in Kierkegaard's view, is not that the poor are absent, or that the preacher has not gone to the poor. Kierkegaard is neither a St. James nor a St. Francis. The tragic thing is that nobody laughs; that nobody sees the comic disproportion between this business of Christendom and what it means to be a Christian; that all are subject to the monstrous illusion of Christianity. This illusion is something different from the deceptiveness present in a Christendom that does not practice what it preaches. Many men in history have undertaken to account for the deceptiveness. They have called the church an invention of priests intent on their own aggrandizement, or a device adopted by ruling classes for the protection of their privileges, or the artifice of slaves seeking to degrade nobility. Others, working as reformers rather than destroyers, have called for the elimination of some deceptions and for the reconstitution of Christianity on the better foundations of right beliefs or of true Christian morality. But all of them have continued to believe that Christianity can be an objective something—a system of teachings, a church, a code of ethics. This is the "monstrous illusion" that Kierkegaard attacks; it is the illusion to which the defenders of the faith and its foes, its conservators and reformers, are equally subject. Though at times he speaks like a sixteenth-century sectarian or an eighteenth-century anti-religious rationalist, accusing the church of only playing at Christianity or of practicing fraud, his chief concern is always to dispel the illusion that Christianity can exist in an objective form or that anything objective can be Christianity. The illusion is that there is such a "thing" as Christianity or that any "thing," be it creed, history, code or organization, can be Christian. Only the subjective individual can be Christian.

A direct, frontal attack on the illusion of objective Christianity only tends to establish it in some other form. Men can only be seduced as it were from their bondage to it. So Kierkegaard practices all his wiles, as well as engaging in outright polemic, to win us away from the hallucination. What sounds like anti-religious polemic is employed for this purpose. His exposure of the hypocrisies in Christendom is used not at all for the sake of establishing it on truer objective foundations, in the form of a better organization, a truer ritual, a more effective program of action, but solely for the sake of winning us away from the idea that objective Christianity can exist otherwise than as an illusion. The contradictions present in objective Christianity are indications of its unreal character.

ON BECOMING A CHRISTIAN

On the positive side Kierkegaard's activity was directed towards the illumination and creation of Christian reality. The fight against illusion was only preparatory to this or its constant negative accompaniment. One must say, "illumination and creation," for the task to which he devoted himself was not only that of calling attention to the hidden subjective reality but of furthering its realization. What is hidden by the monstrous illusion of objective Christendom is subjective existence itself; the essential mark of such subjective existence is that it is endlessly striving to be and to become. Christianity is real only in the form of selves trying to become Christians.

As Kierkegaard's polemic has a double direction—

against the deception in objective Christendom and against the illusion that Christianity can exist objectively—so his constructive activity has a double purpose: that of directing attention to what is truly "objective" to the subjective Christian and that of serving the subjective Christian in his effort to relate himself to his true "object." We may state the Kierkegaardian problem like this: there is a correspondence or, better, a kind of dialogue between the self and the "other"; as the "other" so the self, as the self so the "other." The self that lives in relation to an objective Christianity—i.e. a system, a thing, an "object"—is not an individual self at all but a kind of concretion of the public mind; it is not an "I" so much as a kind of "It." It believes what everybody else who is related to this objective church believes; it hopes what everybody hopes for; it participates in Christianity as it participates in the common language; it does not decide but accepts the decisions made for it by others— the parents and the community that brought it to Christian baptism, the nation that established the state church. But when the "other" is the holy God and Christ the Master then the subject cannot exist as a part of the mass. Or conversely, when the self exists in the precariousness and contingency of its individual selfhood, as self deciding in the *either-or* situations in which its own life depends on its decisions, then the "other" it confronts is the Absolute. When it exists before Christ it is present as this individual subject directly challenged by the question, "Will you also go away?" and forced to decide for itself. What is wrong with the church from this point of view is not that it is not witness to the Absolute and Christ so much as to itself or to the system of Christianity and therefore does not point men to the place where they can become Christians.

The true "other" of the subjective Christian is not Christianity but Christ. To understand Kierkegaard at this point it is necessary, I think, to disentangle two strains in his presentation. To some readers he seems to say that what is wrong with objective Christianity is that it directs men to attend to a Christ who requires no moral effort, a Savior who makes all decisions for us. And there is indeed an important emphasis in Kierkegaard on the strenuousness of the Christian life before the demanding Christ, before Christ who is the Pattern. But the more significant point is not that Christ is *Pattern* rather than mediator of grace; it is rather that *Christ* is the pattern, and no imitation of Christ can be pattern for the Christian. The situation here seems to be like the one with respect to eternal happiness. In that case Kierkegaard had spoken of the Christian as one who is passionately concerned for his eternal happiness. He has been interpreted as meaning that the Christian is a kind of egoistic hedonist, but the emphasis does not lie so much on the word happiness as on *eternal*. Whatever is to be said about man's search for happiness and about Christianity's interest in that search, what must be affirmed of the Christian is that, insofar as he is concerned about happiness, he is passionately concerned about *eternal* happiness. The Christian does not exist as Christian when he seeks both temporal and eternal happiness; he becomes Christian only in the recognition of the incommensurability of the temporal and the eternal and in the decision that he makes between the *either-or* of temporal or eternal felicity. So now in the case of Christ as the pattern, Kierkegaard's intention was to point out that we all have patterns, that we all make our lives works of art. The question is, what is the "object" before the Christian; who is the Master whom he imitates, not as one who copies the masterpieces, but as one who works as the Master works? The deceptiveness of objective Christianity lies in its introduction of other masters or patterns than Jesus Christ. The Christian who imitates an imitation is trying to become or being encouraged to become an imitation Christian. Here again there is an *either-or*: either Christ or not-Christ; either the absolute or a relative.

Before the Christian who is trying to become a Christian there stands in his hiddenness a God who is utterly different from himself; different in his eternity, different in his holiness. There is a great strangeness here, the strangeness of God who becomes man, of the man who is God. Once again we may say that Kierkegaard is a Chalcedonian Christian who maintains that what we have before us as believers is a doctrine, the dogma of the incarnation. But he may be understood more fairly like this: we human beings in order to make things easy for ourselves either project a God who is far off and indifferent to us, or one who is most intimately present, as spirit within, as man himself, or as a kind heavenly Father. But what we have before us in true Christian subjectivity, or what rouses and makes us subjective Christians, is the strange, the anomalous, the incomprehensible one who is far off and nigh, who is utterly different and like ourselves. This is the God who invites and challenges faith.

Insofar as we can point to these elements in Kierkegaard we can say that he was a church reformer insisting that what the state church and the sects needed to do was to become witnesses to the Truth, to direct men away from themselves to the eternal, to Christ, to the ultimate, to the absolute. But now Kierkegaard is most aware of the tremendous difficulty of this reformation.

Here is not something that can be accomplished by
means of a simple resolution. To become witnesses to
this Truth, to be witnesses whose whole manner of
existence points to it is the most difficult thing in the
world. The illusion that this revolution toward the true
object can be accomplished objectively—"out there" in
the church—must be overcome.

Hence his work is directed to the edification of that
Christianity which is hidden and perhaps must always
be hidden in the churches whose function it is to reveal
it or to realize it.

True Christianity as it exists in living subjects, or as
living selves become themselves by becoming true Christians, is a becoming, not being. It is a becoming eternal.
It is a becoming true—becoming a being with only one
aim and that an absolute one.

This becoming a Christian is not a painless process of
growth, or, for that matter, even a growth accompanied
by certain growing pains. It is a becoming by the self of
what it is not. It is becoming what it is not possible for
the self to become. If we say that it is becoming what
it is possible for God to make us become, we must not
forget that it is a becoming of free men who must make
themselves. The paradox of Paul applies: "Work out
your salvation with fear and trembling since it is God
who worketh in you." That *fear and trembling* is one
of Kierkegaard's favorite phrases. The subjective Christian who exists, hidden behind the façade of secure and
established Christianity, is all fear and trembling. And
that is what he ought to be in view of his God-relation.

The real, existing Christianity of subjective selves in
relation to their absolute objects is one of attraction and
repulsion. "All ye shall be offended in me," Jesus said.
And if we are honest we confess that we are indeed

offended by him even as we are attracted. We lie between the poles of this magnet. He draws us to him so that we cannot get away; and he repels us. Or we take offense in him. And when we regard our fellow men—the sincerest among them—we see they are offended too, though in various ways. One can tell where this preacher of the Gospel is offended by what he leaves out as he chooses his text; where that other one is offended by what he puts in; where this theologian is offended by the arbitrariness of his interpretation, that one by his historizing of the text. It will not do to say as the objective church says: "This must not be; you must not be offended by Jesus"; one notices that it also is offended.

Becoming a Christian, which is the only form in which Christianity exists, is an affair of living in the constant pain of repentance or in the repetition of repentance day by day. When one looks at objective Christianity with its ritual and its dogmatic forms it seems as though repentance were a stage through which the soul passed on the way to having become a Christian. Now it is Christian and its sins are forgiven. But that is the illusion. The reality of subjective life in relation to God is the constant repetition of repentance, the daily sorrow over sin, believing today in the forgiveness of sin which was believed forgiven yesterday, and for which the believer expects to repent tomorrow.

As the individual becomes a Christian he believes. But faith is not something that he possesses; it is a constant struggle, a faith renewed and repeated in the face of repeated doubt. It is a faith that has been tried, is being tried, and that will be tried. To believe is not to *be* a believer, but to become a believer in every moment, without confidence in the soul's power to believe, but only with confidence now that tomorrow God will give it faith as a wholly new and wonderful act of grace.

This becoming a Christian, since it is a relation to the absolute, is not a state in which this Kierkegaardian self can now become content, as one tries to do when one says to oneself, "I am becoming a Christian and must be content with my immaturity." For one does not become a Christian at all except before God and therefore always in fear and trembling.

Kierkegaard had a favorite parable for this matter of becoming a Christian or even being a Christian. It is, he says, like lying on seventy-thousand fathoms of water— and being joyful.

Even when we have taken out of the work of Kierkegaard these themes of the monstrous illusion of Christendom and of the task of becoming a Christian many enigmas remain. They are in part, perhaps, enigmas in himself, but for the most part contradictions in our own existence to which he ruthlessly yet like a physician calls attention. First and last we try to get rid of this disturber of our peace. We can each think of a dozen things that are wrong with his analysis, of a dozen things he has left out of the experience of becoming a Christian. And yet, offended as we are by him, it is hard to escape him. It would be as fallacious for us to point to him as a witness to the truth as it was for Professor Martensen to point to Bishop Mynster as such a witness. But he remains in his singular, intrusive way, a witness to the witness. And we remember that even the one he pointed to was the one who said, "If I bear witness to myself my testimony is not true."

3. *Miguel de Unamuno*

In the galaxy of figures who have come to be known as existentialists, one of the most illustrious is too often forgotten. That one is Don Miguel de Unamuno, the sage of Salamanca. Not only is Unamuno worthy of a distinguished place in the history of existentialism; he must be regarded also as one of the very greatest men of letters of the twentieth century.

Unamuno will be associated forever with the Spanish city of Salamanca. As Weimar means Goethe in the world of letters, and Florence means Dante, and the Lake District of England is linked forever to the poets, Wordsworth and Coleridge, Salamanca, on the plain of old Castile, will evoke the memory of Miguel de Unamuno in all future generations.

In the Basque city of Bilbao, which nestles at the foot
of a mountain range on the shores of the Cantanbrian
sea, Unamuno was born in 1864. Save for a few years in
the twenties of the present century, when he lived in
exile from his native country, he resided in Salamanca
from 1891 to the day of his death in 1936. From 1901
to 1914 he was Rector of the medieval university of that
city. There by the banks of a river, the slow-flowing
Tormes, which in his own words, "does not bring or
carry away anything save its waters," Unamuno spent
his best days, with his books and his friends, with his
thoughts and his ceaseless struggle to grasp life's mysterious meaning.

The recent celebration of the seventh centennial of
the University of Salamanca brought back the memory
of Unamuno in a very dramatic way. Unamuno had been
a lifelong foe of Roman clericalism in Spain. In 1914 he
was deposed from his position as Rector of the University
of Salamanca, being subsequently excommunicated by
the Church of his fathers. The edict had gone forth that
no Spaniard taking part in the anniversary ceremonies
should mention the name of a man whom the Church
regarded as "the greatest heretic and teacher of heresy."
Under this ecclesiastical pressure, the University, which
had been all set to honor its greatest son, went into a
sudden panic. Unamuno's old home was to have been
opened as a museum, but the plan was cancelled. Plans
were also cancelled to visit his grave. Invitations to his
relatives were rescinded. Even the mention of his name
in the program was prohibited. But when the visitors
from abroad arrived, they would not be curbed. According to the report of an eyewitness, which appeared in
Time Magazine [1] "they queued up hour after hour to
visit his house, decked his bust with flowers, trudged

through rain and mud to place wreaths on his tomb. Finally, they gathered in the great ceremonial hall, and as each one rose to congratulate the University the forbidden name seemed to pop up again and again and again. At the end of the ceremony, the Rector of the University of Madrid launched into an impassioned eulogy of 'one of the Spanish masters who will live forever long after many generations have died.' The Bishop of Salamanca frowned and lowered his head, but the cheers burst out, and for long moments applause thundered through the hall. Don Miguel had had his day after all."

Speaking personally, I cannot begin to discuss Unamuno without becoming lyrical. To this Spaniard I owe the greatest cultural awakening that ever came into my life. To him I am indebted for a passionate love of Spain, her people, and her culture, which began to be born within me in 1915, and which was destined to become one of the most decisive influences in my life.

I was a student in Madrid when I met Unamuno for the first time. During the Christmas vacation of 1915, I visited him in his study in Salamanca along with one of his former students. Don Miguel showed me his library where were books in fifteen languages. He could not stand translations, so he always learned to read in the original any writer who interested him. He showed me his three favorite volumes which were never absent from his desk: the "Poems of Leopardi," the "Obermann" of Senancour, and the New Testament. It was from his lips that I heard for the first time the name of Sören Kierkegaard. Two years before Unamuno had written an essay entitled "Ibsen and Kierkegaard." In that essay he remarks, "I learned Danish in order to read Ibsen.

I am glad that I learned it for I found Kierkegaard." [2]
Before German scholars had discovered Kierkegaard,
before Karl Barth had come under his influence, that
great Danish thinker, father of modern existentialists,
was known to a Spaniard who lived quietly by the slow-
flowing Tormes, in a medieval city on the Castilian
plain.

Three years later I read a doctoral dissertation before
the University of San Marcs, Lima, the oldest university
in the Western Hemisphere, on the subject, "Don Miguel
de Unamuno, his Personality, Work, and Influence." A
decade later in 1929, on my way from South America to
Scotland, I spent two days with the sage of Salamanca
in his exile in the little French town of Hendaye, close
to the Spanish border. While I was there a significant
incident occurred. One day the sculptor friend who was
making a bust of Unamuno contemplated his handiwork
with consternation. Early in the morning Unamuno had
drawn the figure of a cross on the soft plaster over the
spot which covered the heart.

At the top of a stairway in the University of Salamanca
that same bust now stands in bronze. Nothing could be
more symbolical of the particular type of existentialism
for which Unamuno stood. A cross over his heart, and
not hanging as a decoration from his neck, is the emblem
of Unamuno's lifelong struggle, his "agonia" to pierce
the mystery of human existence. The cross, not as an
adornment, nor yet as a mere symbol of something that
happened once in history, but rather as the emblem of a
ceaseless struggle, is the key to the thought and life of
Don Miguel de Unamuno. Unamuno's existentialism is
best studied and understood when we consider the man
concretely in a dual role, first, as an interpreter of Spain,
second, as a philosopher of life.

THE INTERPRETER OF SPAIN

There is a sense in which Unamuno is the frankest and most thorough going of existentialists. In his view no human being ever thinks with his intellect alone. Thought is a product of the "man of flesh and bone." Unamuno is quite frank in saying that he himself thinks as a Spaniard, and that he cannot do anything else. He even regarded himself as the Don Quixote of Spain, maintaining that for that reason he understood Quixote, and so the Spanish soul, better than did the great Cervantes himself. When I was with him in 1929, he whimsically exclaimed, "At the present time Spain is not at home because Miguel de Unamuno is living abroad"! Unamuno belonged to Spain; in a very real sense he incarnated Spain in much the same way that the soul of Russia was incarnated in Dostoevsky.

The mention of Russia suggests an observation which is relevant to our discussion. To a quite unusual degree the literary production of Spaniards and Russians has been colored by race and nationality. Writers like Kierkegaard and Shakespeare could both have done their major work even though they had not belonged respectively to Denmark and England. This is not so in the case of Dostoevsky and Unamuno. It is a most extraordinary thing that neither Spain nor Russia has really belonged to the cultural tradition of Europe. There is a saying current in Spain that "Africa begins at the Pyrenees." Russia, on the other hand, has belonged more to Asia than to Europe. Both lands have lived on the fringe of Europe, one to the West, the other to the East. While both Spain and Russia have profoundly influenced European history, neither one of these lands

passed through a Reformation. Spain was decisively influenced by Erasmus, but not by Luther; while Russia
escaped even the influence of the Renaissance. Both
countries, however, have been inspired in their history
by a profound Messianic sense. Both also have given
birth to totalitarian regimes. Today Russia is the chief
seat of world Communism; Spain is the chief seat of
Fascism.

No one in the history of Spanish letters has succeeded
in interpreting the soul of Spain in the profound way
tht Unamuno has done. He has unveiled the eternal
Spain. In one of his earliest essays, which might be translated "As Regards Racial Purity," [3] Unamuno emphasizes the fact that to understand Spain one must study
the medieval Romances, the Spanish Mystics, and Don
Quixote. Spain, he has said truly, has always been a
"mother of men and not of ideas." Such tremendous
characters as the Roman Seneca, Ignatius of Loyola, and
St. Dominic were all Spaniards. Velazquez, the most
famous of Spanish painters, was essentially a painter of
men, of men who filled a whole vast canvas.

Taking our cue from Unamuno, the two leading traits
of the Spanish character might be described as *passionate individualism* and *serene universalism*.

1. *Passionate Individualism. The Spaniard is the most
tremendous individualist in the world*. It could even be
said that his unruly, self-assertive human nature was
never tamed even by the Christian religion. In a very
real sense the Spanish soul took Christianity and molded
it to its own likeness. This tremendous individualism
appears in different realms. A Spanish writer, as I have
already suggested, can never be anything but a Spaniard.
The characters of the famous dramatist, Calderon de la
Barca, are all Spanish to the core. Contrast this, says

Unamuno, with Shakespeare whose characters, whether Hamlet, Othello, or Macbeth, do not manifest the slightest tinge of nationality or of race. The same obtains in the realm of art. While the Virgins of the Italian painter, Raphael, have countenances which are entirely universal in type, the Virgins of the Spanish painter, Murillo, all have the faces of lovely Andalusian maids.

Spanish mysticism is equally unique. It, too, is strongly self-assertive. While German and Oriental mystics were satisfied to be absorbed into Deity, the great Spanish mystics tended to absorb Deity into themselves. St. Theresa of Avila, one of the greatest of them all, wanted the nuns in the Order she founded to strive to be "strong men," even to the point of "striking terror into men." Here is a self-assertive masculinity entirely different from the mood of mystics tinged with pantheism, who glory in being lost in God. Most striking in this regard is the sentiment contained in the following lines of St. Theresa:

> "This divine union of love in which I live
> Makes God my captive and my heart free.
> But it causes me such pain to see God my prisoner
> That I die of longing to die." [4]

The symbol of Theresa's mystic rapture is the "transverberation" of her heart. A flaming dart is plunged into the saint's passionate breast by a celestial seraph.

There is, moreover, as Unamuno points out, something extremely unsocial about the Spanish religious nature. It is not by chance that the members of Spanish religious orders were called "monjes" from the Greek "monos" meaning "alone"; while the members of Italian Orders were called brothers, "fratellum."

2. *Serene Universalism.* Paradoxically, however, Unamuno points out, *the Spanish temperament is marked by*

*a serene universalism as truly as it is by passionate indi-
vidualism.* The Spaniard, one might say, is natively
"ecumenical"; he is world-wide by nature. He thinks
in terms of wholeness. The true author of international
law was not the Dutchman, Grotius, as is generally supposed, but a Spaniard, Vitoria. The first polyglot Bible
was prepared by a Spanish cardinal, Cisneros, even
against the will of Rome. And let me add this. Before
the recent emergence of dictators on the Iberian penin-
sula, the publishing houses of Spain produced translations from more languages than could be found anywhere
in the English-speaking world. This also is notable. The
original author of the idea of Pan Americanism was,
strangely enough, the Venezuelan, Simon Bolivar, a true
son of the Spanish tradition. At the time, moreover,
when Franco came into power, the President of the
League of Nations was a Spaniard, Salvador de Mada-
riaga.

Unamuno himself is the best illustration of the native
universalism of the Spanish genius. Without any doubt
he was the best read man of letters of his time. Not only
did he read books in fifteen languages. He was equally
versed in classical and contemporary literature. Few for-
eign students of English ever come to appreciate Robert
Browning, but Unamuno was a profound student of
Browning, and was also acquainted with Walt Whitman.
No foreigner was so well-versed as he in Latin American
literature, even though he never left his native land until
he was exiled from it in his early sixties. He was no less
aware of the significant movements of thought in the
contemporary era.

I know of no more extraordinary case of its kind than
the one I now mention. The first time that the name of
Karl Barth was referred to in a public lecture in the

United States was by Count Herman Keyserling. Yet this priggish German philosopher had never heard the name of Barth until he heard it from the lips of Unamuno. The Count, on the eve of a journey to South America, had sought an interview, for publicity purposes, with Unamuno in his exile. The latter suggested, in the course of their conversation, that he would do well to visit a young German-Swiss theologian who was then teaching in Göttingen, and who, in Unamuno's judgment, was a person of great significance. Having known personally the three men involved, I was able to verify the details of what is here stated. Count Keyserling, who prided himself on his intuitive capacity to absorb everything of representative importance in a culture or a people, had to meet a Spanish exile absent from his own country for the first time in his life, before he became aware of what was going on in his native Germany. In 1929 Unamuno was following with close attention the birth of the ecumenical movement in Protestant circles. He spoke to me at that time, and with great admiration, regarding Archbishop Söderblom of Sweden.

3. *The Two Christs.* It is equally true that *no one has ever offered so profound an interpretation of the religion of Spain as has Unamuno.* He makes the luminous suggestion that in the Spanish religious tradition there have been two representative views of Christ quite different from one another, or, more concretely, two Christs. One Christ is the "Recumbent Christ of Palencia," who is utterly dead; the other is the "Crucified Christ of Velazquez," who never ceases to agonize. The Recumbent Christ of Palencia is an image which Unamuno describes in a famous essay.[5] This Christ is an utterly dead figure, a veritable mass of death. The gruesome image represents Christ taken down from the cross, gory and pallid.

Here, says Unamuno, is "death's eternity," the "immortalization of death." "This Christ," he adds, "will never rise again." Playing upon the Spanish word "tierra," which means both land and earth, he exclaims, "El Cristo de mi tierra es tierra" (The Christ of my land is earth). He then goes on, "Oh Christ of heaven, deliver us from the Christ of earth."

This particular view of Christ gave birth to what Unamuno calls the "coalman's faith" (la fe del carbonero), that is, the faith of a man who gives blind obedience to the church as an institution. The Christ whose symbol is a dead recumbent image passed out of history after having given over everything to the Church. The Church's ideal of absolute obedience, says Unamuno, is expressed in the words of Loyola, "to be like a staff in the hand of a blind man." From this religious ideal is derived the "peace of the sepulcher." All inquiry is stifled. In another of his essays, Unamuno describes a painting which he once saw in a Spanish monastery. The archangel, Michael, is engaged in mortal combat with the devil. The devil holds in his hand a microscope. The microscope is the symbol of inquiry, of looking too closely into things. Satan's possession of that instrument was the cause of the battle!

On the other hand, there is in the Spanish religious tradition what Unamuno would call the *Agonizing Christ of Velazquez*. In his most famous poem, recently translated into English, "The Christ of Velazquez," Unamuno interprets the famous canvas of the Spanish painter as representing the figure of a Christ who is not dead, but is in agony. His viewpoint recalls that of Pascal for whom Christ, "will continue to be in agony until the end of the world." This, says Unamuno, is the Christ who "saved death," who "made death our mother." [6] The

Christ of Velazquez, like the cross which Unamuno drew across his heart, is the symbol of his endless struggle. It is the clue to his particular philosophy of life, his existentialist faith. As a follower of this Christ, he does not ask for light or peace, but only for water, water from the abyss, to give him strength to maintain the struggle. The only peace he asks for is "peace in Christ's struggle," "peace in the midst of war." [7]

THE PHILOSOPHER OF LIFE

What has just been said regarding Unamuno makes it clear how a genuine son of Spain such as he, who had pondered long and deeply upon the genius of his race, and who gloried in the fact that he was virtually Spain incarnate, should be a natural existentialist. Unamuno looked at everything, thought about everything, not merely as a "man of flesh and bone," but also as a son of the Eternal Spain. Believing that a passion for glory and for the eternal was the mark most characteristic of the Spanish race, and being committed to the idea that immortal glory could be achieved not by thought but by action, Unamuno was instinctively an existentialist in the pristine sense of that term. For him a man began to "exist" only when he moved out of himself into something larger than his little world of self-interest, when he responded with abandon to the call of a great idea, a great cause, or to the Eternal Order itself in all its phases. "That man," said Unamuno, "who is not interested in the Eternal is a farce and a deceiver." He recognized, on the other hand, that the moment a man takes up this attitude of commitment he is headed for an experience of suffering and for a firsthand knowledge of the tragic. It should not be forgotten that Unamuno's great book, *The Tragic Sense of Life in Men and Peoples*, was written in 1912, two years before the outbreak of the first World War, at a time when the world was still cradled in the rosy romanticism of the Victorian era.

The particular character of Unamuno's existentialist philosophy can best be studied if we consider his answer to the basic question: What does it mean to be a man? When are human beings really alive? In posing and answering this question we will formulate and consider two propositions which crystallize Unamuno's basic philosophy. The first proposition is: *The fundamental problem of life is vocation,* and the second, *the true meaning of life is agonic struggle.*

1. *Vocation. The fundamental problem of life is vocation.* The perennial problem of man's historical existence, according to Unamuno, and in a very special manner the problem of the contemporary era, is the problem of vocation. In his judgment, our problem today is not the distribution of wealth, but the distribution of vocations. A man becomes truly alive, that is, he begins to "exist" when like the great Quixote, he can say, "I know who I am and what I can be." To a group of young Spanish intelligentsia, Unamuno once said, "Get a great idea, marry it, found a home with it, and raise a family." It deeply distressed him that in the current intellectual tradition of his people, those who claimed to be educated did no more than butterfly over the fields of knowledge. For Unamuno the uncommitted life is like the unexamined life; it is unworthy of a human being. For that reason he regarded it as his special role in the Spain of his time to "toss people into the ocean" as he put it, and take from them every plank, in order that they might learn to swim. "Make yourself irreplaceable," he says toward the close of his

Tragic Sense of Life.[8] He would have a man be the kind
of person that when he passed on people would feel that
there could be no other exactly like him. "Sow yourself,"
he exclaims in one of his most moving sonnets,[9] "cast
the inert part of you in the furrow. You will recover
yourself later in your work." For a man to be truly a
man must work, he must identify himself with something greater than himself, and launch out into the unknown. "Let me die, but let my honor live," says a
Spanish proverb. A true man is a "knight," an "hidalgo,"
(*hijo de algo*) that is the "son of something," namely,
of his works. It is not, therefore, where a man comes
from that makes him a true man, but rather what he
represents, what he has done, and where he is going.

It is an interesting fact that in the Constitution of
the Spanish Republic which was ignominiously betrayed
by the great democracies, it was stated, "this is a Republic of workers of every class." Here is an echo of
the life labors of Unamuno, and of the spirit of the
Eternal Spain, a spirit which was never better expressed
than in the words of St. Theresa, "It is works that the
Lord desires." Could there be any better evidence of the
native existentialism of the Spanish genius and of Unamuno's dictum, "Spain is the mother of men, not of
ideas"? In that part of the world which has been influenced by the Spanish spirit, naked ideas never make
their way in their own light, or in terms of their own
inherent truth. Ideas progress and capture disciples only
when they are presented in incarnate form in the lives of
"men of flesh and bone" who make them inherently at-
tractive. This is something which the business promoters
of commercial and industrial wares from the English-
speaking countries have had to learn the hard way both
in Spain and in Spanish America.

2. *Agonic Struggle. The meaning of life is agonic struggle.* To hunger and thirst after the Eternal, as Unamuno recommends men should do if they are to be true men and fulfill their destiny, means *agonic struggle.* In the thought of Unamuno, the religious man is the only true man, and to be truly religious is "to struggle with God as Jacob did from setting sun to morning dawn." "My religion," said he, is "to struggle with God" (*luchar con Dios*).[10] To such an extent did Unamuno regard struggle to be the essence of life, that he endorsed the famous idea of Lessing that struggle is more important than the achievement of victory. So obsessed indeed was he with the majestic character of struggle ("lucha") that he found it very difficult to accept the true Biblical meanings of "grace" and "faith," and even that of "peace when it is like a river." Christian peace is something which transcends "peace in the midst of war" (*paz en la guerra*). While it is true that in a river's course there may occur the roar of cataracts and the gloom of subterranean caverns, there is also the peace of babbling brooks in the uplands, and of the quiet placid waters which flow anon through green meadows to the sea. What gives peace to the waters of a river is that their bed is made, whether they shoot the rapids or swirl through "caverns measureless to man." This too is Christian peace, the knowledge that whatever betides one is in the will of God. For Unamuno, however, there is no life or peace that is not being experienced in the midst of conscious, ceaseless struggle. In a sense his Iberian soul had never been tamed, never fully "brought into captivity to the obedience of Christ."

In *The Tragic Sense of Life*, Unamuno gives his most complete statement of what lies at the core of human existence. Man, he says, wants to live forever. His heart

craves immortality. It affirms that God exists. On the
other hand, the intellect can never provide adequate
reasons to convince a man that God and immortality are
certain. Thus man's heart and head are in endless conflict. How can this conflict be solved creatively? How
can it give birth to an ethic? Reason offers no hope;
man's heart is wounded by its skeptic barbs.

Unamuno's solution of this problem is what he calls
"transcendental pessimism." "Let life be lived in such a
way," he says in effect, "with such dedication to goodness
and the highest values that if, after all, it is annihilation
which finally awaits us, that will be an injustice." [11]
What he is saying is this. If the universe has no ultimate
place for souls that strive after goodness, then the universe is radically unjust. Here is an heroic ethic, a
determination to do the good even though human reason
may affirm that immortality is no more than an elusive
phantom.

The question has been raised, "Was Unamuno a mystic
or was he not"? There are students of Spanish thought
who say that he cannot be justly classified among the
mystics because he was never really content to put himself calmly and confidingly into the hands of God. He
was too enamored of struggle, too committed to ceaseless striving, too proud of his human effort ever to sub-
mit quietly to the Divine. There is some truth in this.
It is quite evident that one of the things Unamuno failed
to discover in the New Testament is the meaning of
justification by faith. That was something which another
great Spanish heretic, Juan de Valdes did find, and find-
ing entered into the experience of a calm, dynamic peace.
And yet Unamuno, the Spaniard who glorified struggle
and lived the purest moral life in the annals of Spanish
letters, does give us a glimpse at times into his inmost

being. There a peace did reign "which passes understanding." Says he towards the close of his *Tragic Sense
of Life,* "I believe in God as I believe in my friends,
because I feel the breath of His love and the touch of
His invisible hand, which draws me and carries me along
and presses upon me; because I have the intimate awareness of a special Providence and of a universal mind
which shapes my destiny. . . . Time and again I have
found myself on the crossroads of life. Time and again
I have felt the thrust of a sovereign and loving Power.
And then the path of the Lord opens up before me." [12]

And yet even here, there is no sense of perfect calm.
In Unamuno's view, indeed, there is no such thing as
perfect peace in man's historical existence, nor should
there be. He knows of no terrestrial peace such as Bun-
yan's Pilgrim experienced in the "Chamber called
Peace," before his descent the following day into the
"Valley of the Shadow of Death." We are not surprised,
therefore, to learn that on the tombstone which marks
the last resting place of the Philosopher of the Agonic
are inscribed there words from one of his poems:

> "Lay me, Eternal Father, in thy bosom,
>   That mysterious home:
>   I will sleep here, for from life's fierce struggle
>   I come all undone."

4. *Nicholas Berdyaev*

In his latest, posthumously published book, Nicholas Berdyaev remarks: "It is a pity that existential philosophy has become fashionable, and that thanks especially to Sartre. Even Heidegger, a writer to whom access is not very easy, and whom few people have read, has become fashionable. Serious philosophy ought not to be allowed to become a matter of fashion: it just does not suit it." [1]

Berdyaev himself certainly took existential philosophy seriously. In fact, it is so basic to all his thinking, and so many of his concepts in both philosophy and theology are rooted in it, that without understanding his existentialism one cannot understand Berdyaev at all. But he differs from most other existential philosophers in that he derives his initial insights into philosophy and religion from Dostoevsky instead of Kierkegaard.

His existential point of view began to emerge in his thinking in 1912, when he was preparing the most important book of the early stage of his development, *The Meaning of Creativity*.[2] This work represents a crisis in his thinking, the abandonment of his Kantian idealism for the first glimpse of his existentialism. One may henceforth trace the gradual development of this view through most of his subsequent writings. But more particularly are his expositions of existentialism detailed in his *Solitude and Society* (the Russian title of which, *Ya i mir obyektov*—I and the World of Objects—[1934], is far more expressive of the theme of the book than the present English title); *Spirit and Reality* (originally published in 1937); *Slavery and Freedom* (published first in 1939); *The Divine and the Human* (1947); *The Beginning and the End* (the Russian edition, 1947); and the most radical statement of existentialism, *Truth and Revelation* (1953).

EXISTENCE AND THE REALM OF SPIRIT

Berdyaev, in a well-nigh bewildering multiplicity of definitions, and it must be confessed, with a maddening repetitiousness, formulates his concept of existence in sharp contrast to that of being. Ontological philosophies regard being as the highest good, the basis of all reality. The existential philosophy affirms that the subject alone exists, is truly real, not the object which is dependent, phenomenal. Being connotes matter, the phenomenon; existence connotes spirit, the noumenon. Spirit, existence, freedom are primary; being, matter, determinism are secondary. Being emerged into existence only after the

cosmogonic division of subject and object had taken
place. It is a product of thought, or objectification. Thus,
with Berdyaev, the terms "subjective" and "objective"
are far more radically opposed to each other than among
non-existentialist philosophers. Existence "is not essence,
is not substance, it is a free act." [3] Accordingly, contrary
to the generally prevalent idea, being does not tell us
what a thing is, but only that it is. In other words, it is a
predicate, not a substantive. When I say, "God is," the
verb asserts only a fact about God, not what He is. It is,
therefore, a naive error to identify the "objective" with
the "real." Only the existential is real. As Kant demon-
strated long ago, science deals only with the appearance
of reality and can never penetrate to that which is real,
noumenal. This truth, commonplace to all who are even
moderately acquainted with Kantian philosophy, had
been held by Augustine in the form of the distinction
between "Knowledge" and "Wisdom," and is now
shared, although on different grounds, by Albert Ein-
stein. The latter assures us that science can deal only
with the function and interaction of matter, but can
never know or penetrate into the nature of matter.

Furthermore, Berdyaev never tires of characterizing
spiritual reality as freedom. As the objective matter is
governed by rigid determinism, necessity, the existential
spiritual reality exists only in freedom, since freedom is
its principal characteristic.

Thus truth, meaning, are subjective, not objective.
They exist only in the spirit, not in the thing. Truth is
within the subject, not empirically in the object. Truth,
then, is always "supernatural." A thing, the perceived
object, has no meaning in itself; that is supplied by the
perceiving subject. To a cow a chair is a meaningless
contraption, although she knows what grass is for. To an

Australian bushman even a simple mechanism is a
meaningless construct of wheels and levers. To most
non-specialists among educated people a highly complicated machine is similarly incomprehensible unless a
specialist explains it to them. For the meaning of any
mechanism is the function which its designer has built
into it. Knowledge, therefore, even scientific knowledge,
is never merely objective, as John Locke and some naive
modern empiricists think it is. It is a composite affair,
consisting of sensory percepts plus the meaning which we
as perceiving subjects incorporate into it. To that degree
Berdyaev holds that the subject creates the object, or
more correctly, the meaning of the object. Knowledge,
therefore, is not merely passive, "objective," but creative,
active, and to an important degree independent of the
external object.

1. *God.* That being so, the permanent focus of all
Berdyaev's concern is the realm of the spirit, of meaning,
of existence. That is primary, the realm of matter is
secondary, and he leaves it to the scientists. First of all,
then, let us consider this conception of God. Since God
is a Spirit, not *ousia* or *essentia,* He belongs to the realm
of the existential, not of the ontological. He is not a
Being—spelled with a capital "B"—but the Ground of all
being—spelled with a small "b." With this radical statement Berdyaev, the existentialist, boldly repudiates all
the ontological theologies, beginning with those of
Augustine and Thomas Aquinas and including those of
our own day. He insists that the ontological notion of
God is not derived from the Bible but from Aristotle.
He asserts that "God cannot in any sense whatever be
conceived as an object, not even as the very highest object. God is not to be found in the world of objects." [4]
He is always a subject. All the age-long efforts to discover

proofs of His existence "objectively" have failed, as Kant pointed out long ago. There can be no such thing as "scientific" theology, for science deals only with objects, with matter. God does not belong to the phenomenal realm; hence, He cannot be discovered there. He may be known only in the existential encounter, in the "I-Thou" relationship which is primarily that of communion rather than of intellectual apprehension. For spirit with Spirit can meet. Our knowledge of God is, therefore, basically intuitive, subjective, experiential, or, if you will not blanch at the word, mystical. It is neither exclusively intellectual, emotional, volitional, nor intuitional, but rather integral, combining all these four together with the indefinable additional element which results from this integral approach.

2. *Human Personality.* Having considered Berdyaev's concept of God, let us now turn to his teaching about man. Man is also a spirit as well as a body-mind entity, a spirit incarnated in a psycho-physical organism, all these aspects forming a personal unity. The dualistic elements of spirit and body-mind are unified but not obliterated in man. Berdyaev is fond of saying that man is a microcosm, the meeting point of these two kinds of reality. This is man's chief glory, but also the cause of his greatest tragedy. Being a microcosm, man is a subject as well as an object. He possesses a spiritual nature by virtue of which he participates in noumenal existence, although by reason of his body-mind organism he also belongs to the material, objective realm. He is capable of becoming either a beast or a divine-human personality. Since our physical and social sciences sometimes ignore and sometimes even deny the spiritual nature of man, and our secularist culture takes its cue generally from the sciences, our greatest danger today lies in the

degradation, depersonalization of man. Berdyaev's strenuous opposition to this modern heresy constitutes one of his principal contributions to the Christian world-view.

But it must not be supposed that Berdyaev asserts that every individual is a person. Indeed, we owe to him the sharp distinction between those two concepts. The term individual belongs to the naturalistic and sociological categories.

"The individual is born within the generic process and belongs to the natural world. Personality, on the other hand, is a spiritual and ethical category. It is not born of a father and mother, it is created spiritually and gives actual effect to the divine idea of man. Personality is not nature, it is freedom, and it is spirit. It might be said that personality is not man as phenomenon, but man as noumenon, if such terminology had not too much of an epistemological flavour about it." [5]

Thus, for Berdyaev, as for other existentialists, personality is something to be achieved by a moral and spiritual struggle, the highest goal to be attained by a life-time of strenuous endeavor. It is freedom from all external slaveries, social as well as individual. "Man ought to be free, he must not be a slave, for he ought to be a man. Such is the will of God." And going a step further, Berdyaev links up this concept of personality with the ancient Eastern Orthodox concept of salvation as transformation of the human into the divine-human personality. "Human personality," he writes, "is human only when it is divine-human. . . . Human personality is a theandric being." [6]

3. *Freedom.* Passing on, then, from Berdyaev's view of man to his concept of freedom, one must regretfully admit that in this regard he departs most markedly from the traditional Christian doctrine, and stoutly defends what many would call a theosophic view, although he

himself regards it as essentially Christian. He derives it from Jacob Boehme, who speaks of the primeval meonic void as the *Ungrund*. In the beginning (if one is allowed to speak of a beginning) of the cosmogonic and theogonic processes, there existed meonic freedom which is interpreted as an urge to be. Because it was freedom, it contained within itself the possibility of both good and evil. Freedom is, therefore, *uncreated*. Had God created it, He would, according to Berdyaev, be responsible for all its abuse on the part of His creatures, angels and human beings, and for the consequent misery and evil in meta-history and history. For evil is nothing else than the abuse of freedom on the part of man, self-assertion, selfishness. One is reminded of the unknown author of the *Theologia Germanica*, who declared in a trenchant, arresting phrase that "Had he (Adam) eaten seven apples, and yet never arrogated anything to himself, he would not have fallen." [7] Similarly, there is no shaking of Berdyaev from this doctrine of uncreated freedom existing in the meonic void in the *Ungrund*: he stoutly maintained it to the end; in fact, ever more stoutly as the end approached.

It is the abuse of human freedom, then, which produces our "fallen" world in which reign injustice, wrong, oppression, ignorance and sin, and consequently pain and misery. But God did not create this "fallen" world; human beings created it. This corruption which pervades all human conduct—thoughts, aspiration, and actions—Berdyaev calls objectification. This is his principal *bête-noir*. Objectification, as it affects the subject, consists of the loss of personality, of catapulting the person from his own spiritual center and integral unity into the external world, and thus alienating his spirit from itself; the process results in enslavement to the external, be it the mores of society, the compulsion of the state, or individual vices.

This loss of personality is graphically illustrated by Albert Camus in his novel, *The Stranger*. The author delineates the life of a young man whose reactions to stimuli are entirely mechanical, reflexive, impersonal. His mother dies, and he goes through the socially-approved customary behavior without any personal emotional response. A young woman falls in love with him (as the conventional phrase has it, although its connotation is largely physiological), but the young man's response brings him into no emotional or spiritual communion with his lover. He kills an adolescent scamp and is sentenced to death without ever discovering himself, without experiencing what might be called an awakening of personality. Here is a masterful portrait of an individual devoid of personality, whose mental life is a mere stream of consciousness undirected by a personal ego. His psycho-physical organism responds to stimuli in a purely mechanical, Pavlovian fashion. The horror of it is that our secularist civilization accepts the Pavlovian type of anthropology as scientific.

In the second place, objectification consists of treating another person as if he were a thing, a commodity, rather than a potential or actual highest value. Instead of the "I-Thou" communion between one person and another, the objectifying process substitutes rationalization, depersonalization. Kant expressed the same idea when he insisted that man is never a means, but always an end. When industry and economy exist for the sole purpose of benefiting one privileged group in society rather than for the common good of all, and men engaged in it, whether they be workers or managers, are treated as a commodity, as "hands," rather than as persons, this is the result of economic objectification. When political systems, whether totalitarian or democratic, are used for the advantage of a minority, such political abuse is the result of wrong political thinking—another form of objectification. When man treats his fellows with contempt, disdain, prejudice, and discrimination as to their social, racial, intellectual, or even religious status, this is the result of objectification. All these wrong ideas and acts combine to form colossal social wrongs, create monstrous cultural systems of which all members, the innocent with the guilty, are the victims. But all these social evils are man-made. They are the result of wrong ways of thinking which through long periods of time have hardened into customs, mores, civilization. Furthermore, objectification may be viewed as idolatry, as substituting for God and worshipping anything less than God. To worship less than God is to be less than man. Thus, in summary, it is clear that it is we who have created this "fallen" world, not God. And man caught in the wheels of this vast social machine suffers dehumanization, depersonalization. Being regarded as less than a person, he in the end accepts his degraded status. That is the fearful tragedy of modern man.

EXISTENTIAL RECONSTRUCTION IN THEOLOGY

What difference does this existential reconstruction in philosophy, this radical break with the ontology inherited from the Greeks, formulated by Thomistic scholasticism, and refurbished by Hegelian idealism, make in relation to the basic concepts of historic Christian theology? How does it affect them? The effect of existential philosophy is as revolutionary in theology as it is in philosophy. As Berdyaev himself states the case,

"The new path that philosophy is following takes for granted a revision of the traditional philosophy upon which Christian theology and the interpretation of Christianity have rested. . . . The idea of God, of Providence, of Authority, the naively realistic conception of the creation of the world and of the Fall, the notion that a rational ontology is a possibility, all these have been due to that process of objectification." [8]

First of all, then, let us see how Berdyaev reconstructs, from the existentialist point of view, the idea of God. He ironically characterizes the traditional idea by saying that "man creates God in his own image and likeness and puts into God not only the best in his own image but the worst also." Hence, the idea of God has been objectified, rationalized by kataphatic theology: men have imposed their imperfect notions, derived from social or cosmic conditions, upon God. Thus, in the first place, Berdyaev denies that God is the creator of this empirical world. "He is certainly not the cause of the world." [9] Following Jacob Boehme, Berdyaev asserts that the world has evolved from the primordial meonic non-being, as did freedom. In one of his earlier books, *The Destiny of Man*, he still held that the world, but not freedom, was created by God. But in his later writings he denies all creative activity of God, thus relieving God of all responsibility for the evils and calamities incident to this world. He asserts that God "does not act and He is not present in plague and cholera, in the hatred which torments the world, nor in murder, war and violence, in the trampling down of freedom or in the darkness of the ignorant boor." God acts only in freedom, in the good, not in anything which is evil. Nor is God to be thought of in sociomorphic terms as a Ruler, the Absolute, or the Pantocrator. "God is not a master and He does not dominate. . . . The will to power is not a property of His,

He does not demand the slavish reverence of an unwilling man. God is freedom; He is the liberator and not the master." [10] He is not the Aristotelian Absolute or the Augustinian Absolute Being or Will. "God is a God who suffers with the world and with man. He is crucified Love; He is the Liberator." He predestinated no one to eternal damnation and desires every man's salvation. Under all conditions and in this or any other world which might exist, God does everything in His power— short of compulsion and denial of man's free will—to woo man to Himself and thus to save him from the consequences of his own sins. "There is no need to justify, we have no right to justify, all the unhappiness, all the suffering and evil in the world with the help of the idea of God as Providence and Sovereign of the Universe. This is a hard saying. One must turn to God for the struggle on behalf of freedom, on behalf of righteousness, on behalf of the enlightening and betterment of existence." [11]

Furthermore, Berdyaev repudiates the traditional Western views of Atonement. He regards the Anselmic theory as a palpably objectified concept wherein the feudal pattern of justice is transferred to God. "To regard the universal tragedy as a judicial process initiated by an angry Deity against offending man is quite unworthy." [12] Salvation is not a forensic, judicial process, but is a transformation of the very depths of man's nature, a work of divine grace, in which the initiative is taken by God. For "God was in Christ, reconciling the world unto Himself." (2 Cor. 5:19)

Among the topics which, in Berdyaev's view, need rethinking in existentialist terms is the problem of evil. Evil is the greatest mystery in the world when considered along traditional ontological lines. It has caused Russian thinkers, and among them Berdyaev, much anguish of soul. The solution, in the latter's opinion, lies in the realization that evil does not exist in the noumenal, existential reality, although it is certainly and indubitably a fact in the empirical world. Berdyaev cites in support of his thesis Gregory of Nyssa and even Augustine. Thus, although "the world lieth in evil," and evil has the mastery over it, we must not conclude that it has the same existential reality as good. That would be sheer Zoroastrian dualism. Furthermore, evil is spiritual, not material. Matter in itself is not evil. As the Apostle Paul expressed the same idea, we fight not "against flesh and blood, but against the principalities, against the powers, against the world rulers of this present darkness, against the spiritual hosts of wickedness in the heavenly places." (Eph. 6:12) Accordingly, although evil must be resisted, the struggle must be carried on principally on the spiritual, not the material level. This is what our secularized civilization does not comprehend. Evil cannot be overcome by bullets or by a mere exchange of one economic order for another. Victory over evil takes place in the depths of human personality by the transformation of the basic drives of the person, wrought by divine grace and results in the winning of man back to communion with God.

It furthermore follows from these premises that evil cannot exist beyond the confines of this empirical world. In other words, evil belongs to this world and not the existential realm beyond. Hence, hell is not an existential reality, although as a fact in this "fallen" world it is altogether too real, and it would be folly to deny it. But to repeat again what has already been said, it is human beings who created hell by the perverse use of their will, by their objectification. When Dante imagined that the inscription over hell's gate read: "Justice moved my Great Maker; God Eternal wrought me: the power, and the unsearchably high wisdom, and the primal love supernal," [13] he only reflected the medieval objectification of the crypto-Zoroastrian notion that evil is eternal. For Berdyaev, only good is eternal, existentially real.

One could cite many other existentialist reconstructions in theology, but perhaps a brief mention of the most important of these reconstructions, the idea of divine Providence in the sense of cosmic harmony, will suffice. This idea has tortured Dostoevsky as well as Berdyaev. Dostoevsky's Ivan Karamazov, who rejected God, who "returned to God His ticket" because he could not accept this world in which divine harmony is so conspicuously absent, is the embodiment of Dostoevskian revolt against the too facile notion of divine Providence. Berdyaev also shares this feeling. He asserts that the cosmos, i.e., the harmonious divine order does not yet exist, but must be created. It is in its creation that liberated man, by putting an end of objectification, will cooperate.

THE ETHICS OF CREATIVITY

Man's chief task, then, is to achieve liberation from thralldom and enslavement to this fallen world. If our slavery is the result of our own making, of the illusions of our own consciousness, and of the worship of idols we ourselves have set up, our liberation from the slavery will be achieved by a victory over the sway of the false ideas about God, man and the world. In other words, if objectification, to use Berdyaev's favorite term, is the process whereby we have created the Molochs and the other monstrous idols to which we sacrifice ourselves, we may liberate ourselves from them by a return to a spiritual communion with the true and living God and a truly personal way of life with our fellows. Instead of the objective social hierarchies of the economic, social, political, or ecclesiastical order which invariably sacrifice the living person to their utilitarian ends (for they are interested only in the socially useful lie), Berdyaev proposes a *charismatic* hierarchy of spiritual worth and character.

"What is needed is to set humanity, pure divine humanity, a human idea of hierarchy and a charismatic sense of it against the fearful slavery of man in objectified society, against the vampire-like tyranny of inhuman and inhumane hierarchical principles and generic ideas . . . The only thing to set against the servitude of man, which takes the most varied forms, including the forms which are liberal and socialist, is personalism which has noumenal foundations. Such personalism, which is social not individualistic, is a personalism of the community." [14]

In other words, community cannot be created on mere sociological bases. There is no community without communion, without the relationship of a person with other persons on a spiritual level.

This then leads Berdyaev to his oft-repeated emphasis on creativity. The redeemed, transformed man, rescued by God's grace from the slaveries of the "fallen" world and of himself is not saved for his own enjoyment. God desires to use him for the continuation of His own creation, which is the Kingdom of God. For although the empirical world is not God's creation, the spiritual, noumenal realm is. In that sense, we are living in "the eighth day of creation." He might have repeated with the John of the Johannine Epistles, "It does not yet appear what we shall be, but we know that when he appears we shall be like him, for we shall see him as he is."

(1 John 3:2) Thus man, freed from thralldom to his own sins and from the illusions and the idol-worship of this fallen world, must use his freedom creatively for the transformation of this world into the Kingdom of God. But this spiritual process has no relation to the mechanistic notion of "progress" by natural evolutionary means.

Berdyaev is fond of affirming that his existentialism is eschatological (although not apocalyptic), i.e., that it is directed toward the end of history. For without an end, history would have no meaning. "The end is the triumph of meaning." [15] It is the goal, the consummation which alone imparts meaning to humankind's weary story on earth. And since only God can set up a goal for the historical process, all talk of "progress" in natural, mechanical, non-teleological terms is sheer nonsense. This eschatological interpretation of Christianity is connected by Berdyaev with his distinction of three kinds of time: 1) the cosmic, which is mechanical and cyclical in nature; 2) the historical, which is teleological and linear and therefore must have a goal toward which it is directed; and finally, 3) the existential, which is really no time at all, but is eternity in which temporal concepts no longer apply. The world emerged from the meonic nothingness into cosmic time; human history transpires in historical time, although occasionally it is broken through by eternity, as when the eternal Logos "became flesh and dwelt among us." Once in a while a man of rare spiritual insight catches a glimpse of eternity, as did Paul on the way to Damascus or Pascal in the aweful mystical vision which changed his life. History without a goal would be a meaningless passage of time, getting nowhere because there is no place to go. For Berdyaev, then, Christianity is essentially eschatological, teleological, directed toward the ultimate divine goal which will be the aeon of the Holy Spirit. But that era is not to be expected in the immediate future. On the contrary, judging by the preeminent degree of disintegration of our fundamentally divided society, Berdyaev expects rather a recurrence of new dark ages. But after crucifixion comes resurrection.

Nor is the liberated man to sit patiently and passively await the coming of that consummation. He has a part to play in bringing it about. This is his obligation as a liberated, creative being. For "every creative act of man is eschatological in character and brings this world to an end." [16] Every glimpse of beauty, truth, and goodness in nature, man, or art is a partial transformation of the objectified world into the existential reality. It heralds the coming of the Kingdom. Thus the consummation of the goal entails the destruction of the illusions, of the idols men worship, of the false concepts and relations which exist in this "fallen" world. In this future era, all barriers which alienate man from his fellows will at last disappear in "the communion of saints." It will occur partly in time, and partly in eternity.

Such, then, in brief outline, is the existential thought of Nicholas Berdyaev. Many of his glorious visions and poetic insights are inspiring and helpful; some of his ideas will not commend themselves to Christians, whether they be conservative or liberal. Such general acceptance no philosopher or theologian is accorded, nor indeed should expect. But at one point all modern Christians should be profoundly grateful to him: for his impassioned defense of the spiritual nature of man. Our natural sciences, our sociologies, our economic orders, all too often look upon man as a thing, a tender of machines, a robot. He is still necessary for the creation of

economic goods and for the acquirement of riches. But
he has no eternal value. This is the essence of that
modern paganism and nihilism which Berdyaev assails.
As a Christian, I dread to think what is to become of
civilization if this Pavlovian view of depersonalized man
should become permanent. Therefore, I regard the defense of the spiritual nature of man as the central point
of the theology of the future. I believe that the struggle
between liberalism and Barthianism has yielded just
about all the benefit it was ever capable of contributing
to the Christian cause, and I sincerely hope that the
theology of the future will rally to the defense of man's
spiritual nature. As blood rushes to an injured part of
the body to ward off the toxic effect of the invader, so
should the theology of the future rally to the aid of this
imperiled doctrine. In such a theological reconstruction
Berdyaev's lifelong labors in defense of the spiritual
nature of man will prove of the greatest importance and
help.

J. V. LANGMEAD CASSERLEY

5. *Gabriel Marcel*

Gabriel Marcel is an outstanding member of a galaxy of distinguished lay thinkers and writers which is one of the characteristic glories of contemporary French Catholicism: Maritain, Gilson, Thibon, Mauriac, and many others. It is in such distinguished company as this that Marcel's name must be mentioned. On the whole it is true to say that theology and Christian philosophy are less narrowly clericalized in Roman Catholicism than in the non-Roman western churches. This may seem something of a paradox, yet there is no denying the fact that generally speaking in the non-Roman Catholic Christian world the main burden of theological thought and research is borne almost entirely by the ordained ministers of the churches. The front rank lay theologian is nearly always a Roman Catholic.

If this is something of a paradox it is at least an intelligible one. No doubt the compulsory celibacy of the Roman Catholic clergy has something to do with it. Where clerical celibacy is not insisted upon a very important moral and emotional barrier to ordination is removed, and many men enter the ministry who would not do so if their spiritual lives had to be lived in a Roman Catholic context. Normally Protestants who care enough about religion and theology, and are sufficiently equipped intellectually and academically to make reflection upon it, and upon related subjects, the central work of their lives, care enough about these things also to desire to become ordained ministers. In the Roman church this is not necessarily so. Again, the intellectual discipline and pressure to which the members of the Roman church are subjected bears more lightly on the laity than on the clergy, so that there is a distinct advantage, from the point of view of the free development of the best kind of Roman Catholic philosophy and theology, in not being ordained.

Nevertheless Marcel is not entirely immune from the pressure of authority, and it may be noted that since the publication of the encyclical *Humani Generis,* Marcel has declared that he is not an existentialist. Of course the kind of existentialism denounced in *Humani Generis* is not the philosophy which Marcel has at any time professed. It looks as if the tendency of Jean-Paul Sartre and his followers to achieve a kind of monopoly of the term existentialist has been greatly accentuated by the publication of *Humani Generis,* for many Christian and theistic existentialists, who might well have claimed to be the genuine article, are now tending to forswear the name, which is in many ways regrettable. At all events among the leading contemporary existentialist philosophers, only Marcel and Heidegger deny that they are existentialist at all.

It is certainly true that the term 'existentialism' is in many ways a misleading one. It seems to suggest a distinctive 'ism' which is professed and defended by a school of philosophers who are agreed about its general definition. This is very far from being the case. We should perhaps do better to use the plural and speak of 'the existentialisms.' We might add that there are almost as many existentialisms as existentialists. In fact the term existentialism refers not to any distinctive philosophical position or doctrine but to a certain point of departure in philosophy, a conviction that the proper theme of philosophy is the human predicament and the proper method of philosophy the analysis of the experience of self-conscious existence. Thus existentialism, insofar as it is the agreed doctrine of existentialists, is a doctrine which declares to us the point at which it is necessary for us to set out upon our journey, not a doctrine which lays down the direction in which the journey shall proceed or determines the point at which it should terminate.

Of course Marcel's declaration that he is not an existentialist changes nothing. In the sense in which we defined existentialism in the last paragraph, Marcel is an existentialist. Whatever he now calls himself, the change is merely verbal. His thought itself remains unaltered, and it is with his thought that we are concerned in this paper.

Marcel's thinking is of a diffuse and unsystematic character reflecting the breadth of his interests and the variety of his intellectual experience. Thus he is a distinguished dramatist and brilliant musician as well as a philosopher, in his earlier years we might almost have said as much as or even more than a philosopher. He was brought up in a comfortable and cultured home in that atmosphere of serious and ethical agnosticism characteristic of so much that was best and most responsible in the thought and idealism of the second half of the nineteenth century. It was only at a mature age that he turned to Christianity. Thus we find in his journal the following entry, dated March 5, 1929:

"I have no more doubts. This morning's happiness is miraculous. For the first time I have clearly experienced grace. A terrible thing to say, but so it is. I am hemmed in at last by Christianity—in, fathoms deep. Happy to be so, I will write no more." [1]

The language, apart from a certain elegance, is the customary language of evangelical testimony to the glory of conversion and the life-transforming power of the sudden eruption of grace. And yet this is not the conventional conversion story, for the conversion of Marcel is essentially the conversion of a humanist not *from* his humanism to an anti-humane theology but the conversion of a humanist *in* his humanism to God. Thus only two days later in a most characteristic passage Marcel can write like this:

"*March 7th* . . . I have been playing Brahms for a long time, piano sonatas that were new to me. They will always remind me of this unforgettable time. How can I keep this feeling of being entered, of being absolutely safe—and also of being enfolded?" [2]

Thus the piano sonatas of Brahms were the natural and appropriate "psalms and hymns and spiritual songs" through which he poured out and expressed the characteristic joy of conversion. Note too the implicit catho-

licity of the experience. This cultivated Frenchman in
the supreme moment of his life turns to one of the most
typical and representative of all north German com-
posers for his means of self-expression. Because the
Gospel has triumphed the human and cultural barriers
are struck down.

Nor, since his conversion, has he felt it necessary, or
perhaps even possible, to relate his philosophy organ-
ically and systematically to his faith. His philosophical
attitudes and characteristic positions remain very much
as they were prior to his conversion. His personal faith
is in the nature of a leap beyond his philosophy, and
his philosophy retains something of its integrity and
autonomy even within the context of his faith. His position resembles that of St. Thomas Aquinas, who is otherwise a very different kind of philosopher from Marcel.
For Aquinas also faith is a leap beyond philosophy
which does not overthrow and detract from the proper
autonomy of philosophy. To say that faith is a leap, the
taking of a kind of 'existential risk,' is not the same
thing as saying that faith is irrational either in the sense
of sub-rational or supra-rational. Life in time is such that
risks and leaps cannot in the nature of the case be
avoided. In some situations it is rational to leap—as,
for example, from the window of a burning house—and
irrational to refrain from doing so. The 'existential risk'
of faith may nevertheless be a shrewdly calculated risk,
of which philosophy can approve without forfeiting its
autonomy. Such it was in Aquinas and such it is in
Marcel. Marcel's philosophy is compatible with his faith,
and indeed prepares the way for his faith and constitutes
the ground of its intelligibility, both to himself, and to
other men, yet it is never identical with his faith. We
could share his faith without agreeing with his phi-

losophy, and we could agree with his philosophy without sharing his faith.

It is impossible to attempt in a short paper any comprehensive exposition of the views of a thinker so unsystematic in his method, so broad in his range of interests and so diffuse in exposition as Gabriel Marcel. I propose in what follows to consider what seem to me some of the most relevant and important of his teachings in three distinct areas of interest which happen to be areas of major concern for me as well as for him. We will consider in turn Marcel as metaphysician, Marcel as social critic, and Marcel as religious thinker. I say "religious thinker" because in my view it would not be possible to describe Marcel as at any time or in any sense a theologian.

MARCEL AS METAPHYSICIAN

Perhaps no philosopher since Socrates—or should I say the Platonic Socrates?—gives us so clear a picture of the metaphysician at work. For Marcel, as for Socrates, it is life itself that asks the metaphysical question. The preoccupation of so much contemporary philosophy with the mere form and status of metaphysical propositions, considered in abstraction from the vital, existential questions which they at least purport to answer, has done much to obscure this basic fact. Philosophy as many of its living professors practice it is more like a technique for asking questions than for answering them, and it is even prepared to rule out of order those questions which it does not know how to answer. Positivist philosophers in particular behave rather like an investigation and censorship committee determined upon the suppression of inconvenient questions by calling in question and libelling the philosophical integrity of those who insist on asking them. But to censor and suppress human questioning must in the long run erode and destroy human intellectualism. Marcel sees clearly that it is life that asks the metaphysical questions; metaphysical propositions are at least attempts to answer questions which existing human beings cannot help asking. In this sense man is by nature a metaphysical animal. Thus even children ask metaphysical questions. Indeed, in our culture it is above all children who ask metaphysical questions, for we have created and to some extent perfected an elaborate educational technique which aims at conditioning us against asking the questions which our reigning intellectualism does not know how to answer. The contemporary preoccupation with subtle and ingenious conundrums about the form and status of metaphysical propositions fails to observe that it is an analysis of the existential reality and inevitability of metaphysical questions which provides the proper context in which to consider the problem of the validity of metaphysics.

Metaphysics is what happens when an existing being, who not merely exists but exists for himself and as a problem to himself, indeed as a mystery to himself, questions not the obvious fact but the obscure meaning of his existence, and that is precisely what none of us can help doing at some time or other.

Thus, to give an example of his method, Marcel visits a sick and dying friend. He is overwhelmed by pity and sympathy for his friend's forlorn condition and as he departs he promises, "I will come again next week." But afterwards he asks himself by what right the empirical self of today thus binds and engages the as yet nonexistent self of next week. Perhaps next week he will not

be in the same sympathetic frame of mind and will not
even desire to visit his friend. Is the existing empirical
self of today perhaps unjustly condemning the nonexistent self of next week to a show of insincerity? It is
in such a manner that he approaches the problem of
continuing personal identity. Man is essentially a being
who commits and engages his own future. Marcel is very
fond of quoting Nietzsche's remark, "Man is the only
being who makes promises." We can see at once that the
metaphysical question about man is raised by marriage,
by ordination, by the religious life in the technical sense
of the word, and by all those solemn acts of the human
spirit in which a man deliberately binds himself to other
men in a specific way of life right up to death itself.

It is notable that Marcel never insists, like Sartre, that
existence precedes essence. The vogue of Sartre has
created a widespread impression that this is the basic
affirmation of all existentialist philosophy. This is not
really so, however. Such a view is not to be found in any
of the earlier existentialist philosophers and Marcel is
not the only contemporary existentialist who rejects it.
The important point for him is not so much to affirm
the metaphysical priority of existence as to recover the
sense of existence. In his view men for the most part
have lost the sense of existence, and it is the function of
philosophical reflection to restore it. Most men think
of life simply as an accidental "happening to be" in a
context that conditions and controls them. Not a little
of our contemporary philosophy and psychology is an
articulation of this fundamentally apathetic point of
view. Thus positivism forswears any metaphysical probing into the meaning of human existence in favor of a
reverent and deferential scrutiny of the immediate
human condition, and not a few psychologists are greatly

given to glib talk about 'well adjusted' personalities, and
so on, which really means, if it means anything at all, a
sychophantic surrender of human existence to what appears to be the contemporary human condition. To recover the sense of existence is thus more than merely to
affirm its priority over essence, rather it is to re-explore
the true meaning of the human essence, for essence, we
may say, requires and necessitates existence. The point
of departure for Marcel is thus not existence itself as
immediately given, but the present incompleteness of
our mode of life. Our world, the world of our culture
and consciousness, is in his graphic phrase, "a broken
world." We can only recover our sense of existence by
a new exploration of the mystery of existence.

This leads us to Marcel's important distinction between
mystery and problem. Problems are always of finite
dimensions. They are inherently fathomable. We wrestle
with a problem, solve it at last, and the problem for us
is a problem no more. Thus the peculiar excitement and
joy of probing a problem occurs only once. That is why
it is impossible to recover the original pleasure and
thrill of a detective novel by re-reading it. Once we know
that it was really the butler who murdered the countess
by pumping poison through the plug hole while she was
taking her bath, the earlier chapters which seemed to
point so conclusively to the guilt of the Archbishop no
longer deceive or intrigue us. Our only hope is to put
the novel aside for ten years or so, by which time we
may perhaps have entirely forgotten it. Though even
then the danger is that we shall suddenly recall the solution three chapters from the end, and the whole climax
will be completely spoiled for us. Mystery, on the other
hand, cannot be solved. We can learn to live with it more
and more significantly, and to penetrate more and more

profoundly into its nature, but however deeply we enter into it and discern its secrets the mystery remains mysterious. It has a certain bottomless and unfathomable quality. Thus we often talk about what we call 'the problem of evil,' whereas what we usually have in mind in such discussions is really 'the mystery of evil.' Although a great deal that is significant and important has been written and said about the so-called 'problem of evil,' it cannot be claimed that the burden of enduring evil, the strain of being compelled to live with evil and the shame of knowing oneself to be evil have been in any way decreased by even the wisest and profoundest remarks of even the greatest philosophers. There is a sense in which we can validly talk about the problem of evil, and that, significantly enough, is the one sense in which the Christian man can intelligibly claim that the problem has been solved by Jesus Christ, and is therefore in principle soluble by us in and through Jesus Christ. The true problem of evil is not the speculative problem of making sense of the fact of evil in terms of a Christian theodicy, but the problem of learning so to live with evil and to endure its sting without reciprocation that faith may not be confounded, hope extinguished, and charity transformed into bitterness and hate. That existential problem Christ solved triumphantly on the cross. The mystery of evil, on the other hand, can indeed be penetrated by adventurous rational speculation, and many valuable insights glimpsed in the process. But although thought can interrogate the fact of evil, and probe into its subtle relationships with other facts, thought can never hope to get to the bottom of the mystery. This is because evil appears within and is indeed a part of the system of contingent reality. Contingent reality is of its very nature inherently mysterious.

Marcel's thought here is very close to the basic insight of Butler's *Analogy of Religion*. In effect Butler replied to the kind of intellectual and theological program of the eighteenth-century rationalists and deists summed up in Toland's slogan, "Christianity not mysterious" by saying, "Not only Christianity but everything else is mysterious." To have one's thought hedged about and ultimately frustrated by mystery is the inevitable consequence of keeping one's thought concentrated on reality. Vico made substantially the same point in his criticism of Descartes, which provided him with the clue to the discovery of his 'new science.'

This distinction between problem and mystery is perhaps Marcel's most important contribution to metaphysical thinking. It does not of itself, of course, amount to a metaphysical system. It does not even clearly indicate to us in what direction we must look for a metaphysical system. It certainly does suggest, however, that it is useless for us to put any trust in the Cartesian conception of a rationalistic system, which identifies the rational with the lucid, the 'clear and distinct.' Lucidity is in fact a semantic rather than an intellectual quality and virtue. The lucid may be quite irrational, whereas many of the highest achievements of reason may defy our attempts at lucid expression. But this, although an important observation, does not supply us with a metaphysical system. Marcel, like Socrates, provides no more than a method and point of view in metaphysics. Marcel, as we have seen, does not concern himself with abstract logical and semantic discussions about the possibility of metaphysics. His task is to vindicate the necessity of metaphysics by weaving a set of continuous variations based on the theme that man is by nature a metaphysical animal.

How does Marcel conceive the human reality? The answer to this question will help to bring out the original and profoundly Christian character of his existentialism. For some, for example for French thought from Descartes to Sartre, the essential human reality is defined and understood in terms of its egocentricity. "Cogito ergo sum." Man is essentially the being who exists for himself, the *pour soi*, whose only choice is that between the robust and the heroic self-assertion which enables a man to obey the dictum of Polonius, "To thine own self be true," or to atrophy his ego in a second hand 'inauthentic' existence, living and moving and having his being in an all pervading atmosphere of 'bad faith.' From this point of view the human reality is conceived primarily in terms of reflection. Men are locked up in the contemplation of themselves like Aristotle's 'prime mover.' An alternative view is provided by Martin Buber. For him the characteristic human reality is found in the *I-Thou* relationship in which men confront each other not as active subject and passive object but as two subjects each recognizing the other's subjectivity. Marcel goes further and penetrates, I believe, even more profoundly into the heart of the human reality. For him the essential human reality is expressed in the first person plural pronoun, *We*. Man is not an isolated solitary existence. The human reality is our personal participation in the corporate human existence. This approach takes up and affirms all that is true and important in the doctrines of Sartre and Buber. Thus, for example, the egocentric type of existentialism does indeed define the nature of the form of being that is capable of participating in the 'we-reality'. The *We* is essentially not a group which is only a group because it has been grouped, not a collectivity which has been collected. The 'we-reality' is essentially a group which groups itself, which constitutes its own existence by affirming its own existence, in an affirmation which imposes a burden of responsibility and fidelity upon all those who make it. Only a being who exists for himself is capable of incorporating himself into the 'we-reality' and yet, and at the same time, only within the context of the 'we-reality' can he become sufficiently aware of his own existence to begin to exist for himself in his integrity. Again, the *I-Thou* relationship so carefully analyzed by Buber is a type of relationship that exists within the *We* and indeed goes very far towards the constitution of the *We*. We may say that the *I-Thou* is an inescapable dimension of *We*. Yet the *We* transcends the *I-Thou*, not merely because of its greater ethical and spiritual significance, but also because of its logical priority—perhaps, we might even add its eschatological posteriority. '*We* are the alpha and the omega —the first and the last.' Some reference to the doctrine of the trinity tempts the writer quite irresistibly at this point, for this conception, the crowning story of Christian theology, is after all the ultimate existentialism, the *ism* which dimly apprehends and humbly ventures to define the ultimate existence. The *I-Thou* is thus a kind of abstract analysis of the more concrete *We*. We may liken it to an analysis of changes within an organism which employs the methods and principles of inorganic chemistry.

We may conclude this phase of our discussion by saying that for Marcel the human reality is neither an interminable solo, nor a chaos of mutually irrelevant duets, like that which assails the ears of the man waiting for a friend in the corridor of the music school, but a vast chorale, in this broken world, alas, always inefficiently and discordantly rendered.

MARCEL AS SOCIAL CRITIC

Marcel himself has described his own point of view as a fundamental rejection of all abstraction.

"The dynamic element in my philosophy, taken as a whole, can be seen as an obstinate and untiring battle against the spirit of abstraction." [3]

It is important not to misunderstand his meaning here. The sin of abstraction is not the mere use of abstract concepts. We abstract in order to give our thinking an often necessary generality and an always desirable clarity. A well-known cliché distinguishes the 'clear and concrete' from the 'vague and abstract.' The procedure of this distinction rather resembles that of our divorce courts. It puts asunder those whom God has joined together, and then encourages the sundered elements to contract two completely incompatible and metaphysically illicit alliances. 'Vague and concrete' and 'clear and abstract' is the proper way of matching up these four characters in the ideal happy ending. The abstraction is clear because it conforms precisely to its definition. The concrete reality is vague, not only because it cannot be defined at all, but also because it inevitably transcends even the most detailed description. A triangle is a crystal clear concept. A friend or a wife is a vague reality, because indefinable in principle and inapprehensible in practice.

The sin of abstraction is not the act of abstraction in itself, but the subsequent metaphysical error of treating our abstractions as if they were concrete realities, rather than intellectual counters and dialectical conveniences. Men create a language of abstract thought and then so mistake its nature as to suppose that it refers to concrete realities. The human mind speaks many languages, and this is all to the good, for only so can it learn to do justice to the many distinct phases of reality and experience. But the multilingual human intellect must be careful not to confuse its languages. We may compare the sin of abstraction, defined in this way, to the basic error of the fundamentalists, who receive and venerate the language of evangelical testimony and the symbolic speech of the religious poet and then interpret it as though it had the directness and matter of fact character of a news item in the *New York Times*.

For Marcel the sin of abstraction is in particular the vice of the technologists, and among the technologists the peculiar failing of those by whom the ordering of society and the world of human relationships is interpreted as primarily a technical problem. Marcel traces this fundamental philosophical error particularly in the totalitarian social orders of our time, in and for which men are primarily functional agents, welfare units, cannon fodder, party members, anything that is abstract and definable rather than human beings. It is important to add, however, that he does not make any fundamental distinction between the totalitarian societies and the modern mass democracies. He is less concerned than thinkers in America and Britain to distinguish between societies as possessing or not possessing the familiar institutions of modern political democracy.

There is perhaps a useful warning to be gleaned from his thought at this point. Sociologically and humanly speaking our own social order may perhaps resemble the social orders which we reject on political grounds more closely than we care to contemplate. This is perhaps not altogether surprising, for both the totalitarian and the democratic states are in our world mass industrialisms, and the characteristic social and cultural consequences of mass industrialism are substantially the same even within the context of strikingly differentiated political structures.

Marcel sees clearly that the root causes of the dehumanizing maladies which afflict and are characteristic of contemporary Western society preceded in time the emergence of both mass democracy and the totalitarian state. For Marcel man's alienation from his own being in the modern world, and his consequent tendency towards an apathetic acquiescence in his brutal and brutalizing immersion in the life of the mass, is to be traced to the earlier preoccupation of the western bourgeoisie with property. For him the traditional preoccupation of the middle classes with property is a tragic substitution of *having* for *being*. He has devoted considerable attention to this contrast between being and having. To sacrifice being for having, that is to interpret, or rather misinterpret, being or well-being in terms of having, is to sacrifice a reality for the sake of an illusion. As Marcel's analysis so profoundly reveals, having is always and fundamentally an illusion. When we think we *have* is precisely the moment when in fact we are *had*. Property controls and de-personalizes the lives of the men who make it their greatest good. This is after all a familiar New Testament theme. Such a pre-occupation alienates men from their own being by alienating them from each other. Thus for Marcel the troubles of our times will not necessarily be brought to an end by a resolution of the conflict between the totalitarian and democratic states in favor of either party. The root of the trouble lies deeper. The proof that this is so, if any proof is needed, may be seen in the way in which two of the profoundest and most prophetic spirits who flourished in Europe a century ago, Sören Kierkegaard and Alexis de Tocqueville, not only perceived and diagnosed the presence of the corrupting germ, but also foretold what the later visible symptoms would be. Marcel as social critic stands in the same tradition as these two great prophetic figures.

On the other hand, it is important to emphasize that Marcel does not suppose, like so many of the more superficial social physicians, that the property-sick patient can be cured by lavish injections of socialization. Marcel sees clearly that socialism is no true alternative to the bourgeois preoccupation with property. Socialism is in fact no more than the distinctively proletarian way of being preoccupied with property. The distinction between bourgeois capitalism and proletarian socialism has in fact been greatly exaggerated by superficial observers of the struggle, and over-excited participants in the struggle. Deep down the two are spiritually akin. Both equally subordinate being to having, both are equally weighed down by a fundamental alienation from the true human reality which any serious existential philosophy is concerned to depict. It is at this point perhaps that we begin to glimpse the subtle way in which an existentialist interpretation of human life begins at last to resemble the old prophetic doctrine of natural law, of the reality and persistence of man as God made him which is outraged by and ultimately compelled to react against the various forms of the human condition which man constructs for himself.

Thus Marcel's social analysis points beyond the conflict between democracy and totalitarianism, and beyond the conflict between capitalism and communism. For him there can be no resolution of the problem of contemporary man, that is of man in an industrialized mass society, on the superficial levels on which these two conflicts take place. His analysis probes the problem on a deeper plane, and his prophetic vision pierces beyond contemporary political horizons. It is true that to wrestle with a problem with so radical a realism as this leaves us at last with a message which cannot be articulated or expressed in contemporary language, and imagery, a diagnosis without a programme which unmasks the guilt of the conservative and lays bare the vanity of the activist 'world-improver.' In the last resort a prophet who is not a poet must keep silent, and the prophet who is a poet cannot be understood. This after all was the perennial dilemma of the Hebrew prophets. There is perhaps only one way of resolving this particular dilemma: Let the prophet but die in Jerusalem, and he will not have lived in vain.

MARCEL AS RELIGIOUS THINKER

Strangely enough it is in this sphere of his thought that Marcel is most of all scrappy and unsystematic. Yet the Christian elements, intuitions and inspirations are everywhere evident, even in his writings before he became a Christian. Here I shall attempt to do no more than indicate three persistent elements in his thought whose relationship to Christian doctrine and experience is particularly clear and significant.

1. *The We-reality.* His persistent stress on the *We-reality*, the conception of personal existence as *par excellence* existence in and for the corporate personal body, so that life for him without the others, all the others, is essentially life in a broken world. Such a conviction has surely been fostered and deepened, if not originally in-

spired, by his experience of life in the church, the
essence of which is summed up and concentrated in our
participation in the liturgy. It is not always easy, I think,
for Christians who have been born and raised in those
areas of Christendom accustomed to non-liturgical worship to achieve any sympathetic understanding of all that
the liturgy means to the best and most spiritually
awakened catholics. The liturgical revival in the catholic
world is not just an archeological revival, though it has
and honors its archeologists: rather it is a true and profound movement of the spirit that expresses itself
through its prophets. It is in the liturgy that such men
savor the quality of the Kingdom of God, and therefore
in the liturgy that they trace the authentic outlines of
social order, and experience that special vision of the
meaning of human existence which a Christian existentialism labors to articulate.

The whole substance of Marcel's profound humanism
may be identified with such intuitions as these. Like the
call of Isaiah, and not a few of the psalms, this experience is essentially a vision which takes place during the
performance of the liturgy, a vision whose liturgical context is in no way accidental, for it is essentially a vision
of what the liturgy truly is and means. For Marcel the
supreme value of human existence is to be found in this
possibility of existing for and in the others, of being
loved by the others, and, above all, by God the Ultimate
Other, who himself transcends that otherness in the loving act by which he makes himself our kin. Men matter
because they matter to each other; all men matter because they matter to God. Human existence is significant
not because of what it is in and for itself, but because
of what it is in and for the others. This is close indeed
to the whole meaning of Christianity, and of that mys-

terious charity which animates not only the Kingdom of
God but the very Godhead itself.

2. *The Mystery of Incarnation.* Again and again in
Marcel's writing we find a profound concentration on
the mystery of Incarnation. For him the only existence
and spirituality which we know is essentially an Incarnate spirituality and existence. The making of man was
the making of man flesh. His religion is thus always and
essentially a faith in and response to the Word made
Flesh, a word made flesh not only or primarily in the
historic incarnation, but also in the church, in the sacra-
ments and in the Christian spirituality incarnate in the
flesh of Christian men. The language of catholic faith
and piety is thus for him the natural language not only
of his orthodox religion but also of his existentialist
philosophy. He moves about in such a world with an air
of complete intellectual and spiritual at-homeness which
is an enjoyable and enviable spectacle. Incarnation so
understood, of course, tends not towards the degradation
of the spirit—as so often in Plato—but towards the glori-
fication and exaltation of the flesh—as in the New Testament and the liturgy.

3. *Fidelity and Hope.* Lastly we may mention Marcel's
preoccupation, particularly marked in his more recent
writings, with fidelity and hope. Almost alone among
contemporary existentialists Marcel returns again and
again to the theme of hope. The hope of which he speaks
is not the hope that we cannot help hoping, nor is it the
hope for what we regard as a rational possibility; it is a
hope essentially based on fidelity, fidelity to God and to
each other. Man, for Marcel, as we have seen, is essentially a being who pledges himself and exhibits his own
unique glory and dignity in his faithfulness to his
pledges. That is why, for example, divorce is so inher-

ently degrading and sub-human. Apparently even the gorillas and the chimpanzees, in the wild state where they have not been led astray by the force of human example, will have nothing to do with any such thing. The divorce court ranges man with the lower anthropoids, and unfavorably distinguishes him from the higher ones.

But fidelity is impossible without trust and hope. Indeed it is fidelity which is above all the element in human existence which opens up the human reality to the pressure and impact of the divine reality.

"It is in this way that fidelity reveals its true nature, which is to be an evidence, a testimony. It is in this way, too, that a code of ethics centered on fidelity is irresistibly led to become attached to what is more than human, to a desire for the unconditional which is the requirement and the very mark of the absolute in us." [4]

Marcel may thus be described as preeminently a Pauline philosopher of faith, hope and charity: faith in Christ, hope in God, and charity in the church, which is the great creation and inspiration of the spirit of God. And for him, as for St. Paul, "The greatest of these is charity." For it is only in and by participation in that collective, living charity which we call the church that we discover the reality and meaning of our own personal existence.

ERICH DINKLER

6. *Martin Heidegger*

There can be no doubt that Martin Heidegger is not only the representative of existentialist philosophy but also one of the outstanding philosophers of our time. To write about Heidegger means necessarily to enter a discussion. A discourse on Heidegger necessarily includes the reader's participation in the question and in the questionability of the topic. Here, as with all historic phenomena, we cannot deal with our topic from a so-called objective distance. As hearers we must become a part of the question, participating in it in order to experience how problematic and perhaps also how relieving our subject is. Only when participating do we escape the trivial mode of being mere beholders, who register facts and who argue about facts. Participation in Heidegger's problems means: to listen to him as an individual, to be open to his thought, and to be without preoccupation, yes, first, to get acquainted with his categories of thinking and to adjust our language to his peculiar way of speaking. This is indispensable, particularly when translating Heidegger's German vocabulary into another language. Heidegger's German language is based upon a very peculiar use of the words, harking back to their original meaning. Since his rediscovery that language and terminology are basic problems of thinking as such, language for him constitutes not only a general problem, namely to formulate the nucleus of ideas, but a very specific concern.

THE MAN AND HIS WORK

Who is Martin Heidegger? Let me cite a few biographical notes. He was born in 1889. The son of a country craftsman from the Black Forest in Germany, he was born in Messkirch-Baden and studied Catholic theology and philosophy at Freiburg University. When twenty-six years old he became a docent at Heidelberg University. His first book dealt with "Duns Scotus' doctrine of categories and meanings." Already in this treatise insights are suggested which became evident later, in particular the theory that truth can only be experienced by "transcending the this-worldly realm." In 1922 Heidegger became full professor at Marburg University and then in 1928 at the University of Freiburg. Today he lives in a small village in the Black Forest, in Todtnauberg. To be a thinker in Todtnauberg today means very much the same as it meant sixty years ago to be a thinker in Sils-Maria, the remote residence of Nietzsche. It means to think about reality outside of reality, to think

about Being as such far away from concrete being.
Whether or not this is an advantage I will not discuss
here.

The book which marks Heidegger's position within
and against contemporary philosophy is entitled *Sein
und Zeit* (1926), or Being and Time. What Heidegger
intended was to outline "fundamental ontology." The
thoughts of today's Heidegger, however, are moving on
different roads. He calls them *Holzwege* (1950) : trails
through the woods, or even beguiling jungle trails.

"In the woods are paths which of a sudden are over-
grown and end in the impenetrable. Then they are called
jungle trails. Each wanders apart, yet in the same
woods. Often it seems that one is the same as the others.
But it only seems so. Woodsmen and forest rangers
know the trails. They know what it means to be beguiled
by a jungle trail." [1]

With such words Heidegger illumines and at the same
time darkens the impact of his book. Indeed, our thinker
approaches the realm of the poet and sometimes enters
the realm of religion. We shall see very soon how this
"change" in Heidegger's language means also a "turn" in
his thought. Yet it would be wrong to understand *Being
and Time* as a starting point and the *Holzwege* as the
conclusion of a systematic progression in this direction.
Thinking in that case would be but a seeming motion,
knowing from the very beginning the final result. Philosophy would fall or remain within the error of construct-
ing a tower of Babel by means of seeming results. However, philosophy as an action of thinking means to be
on the way, means a permanent quest like that of wan-
derers in the forest. It may be compared with constant
digging which aims to dis-close the closed-up Being.
Philosophy, according to Heidegger, has to lay bare the

truth of Being (ἀ-λήθεια, literally the uncoveredness, the revealment of Being). With the aim of disclosing Being in the light of truth, Heidegger more and more approaches the realm of religion. Perhaps we may say about him what he says about the true poet: "He is on the way in the footprints of the Holy." [2]

An in-between station of this way appeared a few months ago when lectures delivered in 1935 were published under the title *Introduction Into Metaphysics*. For foreigners this is perhaps the most readable book by Heidegger, perhaps the only one fitted for translation. These lectures show that Heidegger even in 1935 was on a turning road, that already he had turned to the problem of Being as such as *the* question of Western European thinking. In these lectures it becomes especially evident how far for Heidegger the ontological metaphysics as an action of thinking are rooted in the basic criticism of our present age and of Western history. Heidegger writes: "The Europe of today in fatal disorder, constantly ready to commit suicide, is squeezed between Russia on the one side and America on the other. Seen metaphysically Russia and America are not heterogeneous; both are representatives of boundless techniques and mass organizations of man as a type deprived of his individuality. When the remotest corner of the globe has been conquered and exploited . . . when any event at any place and at any time is accessible, when time is nothing but speed . . . when boxing champions are considered as the heroes of the nation, and when mass attendance of meetings is the top aim—then there is still in the background of all this, like a ghost, the challenging question: what for? what to? what then?" [3]

Europe is squeezed within pliers and suffers from the

fact that she has forgotten what Being as such means. More dying than living between East and West, Europe must learn again to understand herself, out of her own tradition, and to develop from within her spiritual forces. The destiny not only of Europe but of the entire globe depends on what answer is given to the question: "Is Being a mere phrase without deeper meaning, or does Europe comprehend and conceive in this term 'Being' her spiritual destiny? . . . Europe's situation is so fatal because it results from her own disarmament of the spirit, prepared in earlier times. This is a result of her spiritual situation in the first half of the nineteenth century." The so-called collapse of German idealism is a protective and very kind formula which covers a far deeper and older spiritual void. Human beings slipped and slid into superficiality. Surface—dimension—extension—mass routine have become destructive powers, and suddenly "quantity is evaluated as a quality in itself." [4] Saying all this in 1935, Heidegger attributes to Western Europe the decisive responsibility for the disarmament of the spirit and the obliviousness to Being as such. In these passages the influence of Friedrich Nietzsche and Oswald Spengler is obvious.

Yet the cause of modern lostness is attributed to the obliviousness to Being which begins already with Plato. Plato has veiled the very truth of revealed Being by an "idea," thus preparing the way for the falsification of Being in *subjective conceptions*, leading up to Nietzsche. It was this falsification, from which according to Heidegger, philosophy as a genuine thinking about Being decayed into a science (*Wissenschaft*), turning against its true nature. Pretending to be a science, philosophy dealt with objects and thus objectified truth. Yet "philosophy has no object because it is an action of thinking and an event in itself. Only within this occurring event does philosophical truth open up." [5]

EXISTENTIALISM AND EXISTENTIALIST ONTOLOGY

Within the frame of our study we can point out only a few examples of how Heidegger tackles his task of "making the truth of Being speak." [6]

I have selected two topics which overlap and complement each other. Like most of Heidegger's writings they are variations of one theme. The two are: (1) Human being and existence; (2) History and Historicity. But before outlining Heidegger's complex way of thinking in some kind of "woodcut," I must issue a warning. Heidegger has a very peculiar way of speaking and uses a vocabulary of his own. Lord Macaulay once wrote in his diary about Kant's *Critique*: "I tried to read it, but found it utterly unintelligible, just as if it had been written in Sanskrit. Not one word of it gave me anything like an idea, except a Latin quotation from Persius . . . it seems odd that in a book on the elements of metaphysics . . . I should not be able to comprehend a word." [7] This was said about Kant. One is reminded of it when dealing with Heidegger for the first time. Even for Germans he is at first almost entirely a sealed book.

1. *Human Being and Existence.* We have to wrestle first with Heidegger's terminology. Our point of departure, as we have already mentioned, is Heidegger's judgment about our present age, namely about us, men of today, who live on the surface. Our main categories are extension, quantity; we have become standardized types, clinching ourselves to the trivial world of facts. This phenomenon is the outcome of the fact that we comprehend only sheer factuality as Being, that we are not

moved at all by the question: What is Being? Why is Being and why not rather Nothing? And yet: man is the only concrete being capable of asking this question about Being as such. Man is thus a privileged being, privileged through his capacity to ask about Being, which demonstrates his participation in or determination through Being. Ontologically Heidegger defines this privilege of man by the term *"Dasein,"* i.e. literally "being there." With Heidegger we have three ontological terms, which are consistently distinguished from each other. The three terms are meaningful and adequate in the Greek and German languages, but cannot be translated equally clearly into English. Therefore I present a definition: First, *Being as such* or pure Being or absolute Being, i.e., *das Sein,* i.e. τὸ εἶναι. Second, *Concrete being,* i.e. *das Seiende,* i.e. τὸ ὄν. Third, *Human being,* i.e. *das Dasein,* i.e. the human being here and there. In this study we shall use the three terms *Being as such, Concrete being,* and *Human being* in order to preserve the ontological significance involved in the terminology.[8]

We said: only our Human being is privileged to ask about Being as such because only man is capable of understanding himself as related to Being as such. Man alone in his being here and there is concerned with Being as such. Therefore, Heidegger's first step is to analyze and define Human being with regard to the leading question of Being as such. We may interpret: Heidegger demands a philosophical anthropology in order to establish a basis for his ontology, for his thinking of Being as such.

We saw that according to Heidegger Human being somehow always is related to Being as such. Whenever a Human being is aware of this relatedness to Being as such, whether it is affirmed or rejected, Heidegger calls this individual Human being: *existence*. This term existence is not only another word for Human being (Dasein) nor is it a general quality of man. Rather, it may be called a constant *possibility*, namely to be one's self or not to be one's self.[9] This possibility reveals itself to man in the claim and call of Being as such. Our response to this claim cannot be understood as a plan which we choose on the basis of intellectual insight. However, it must be responded to by a *decision*. It must be my own decision to keep alive this relatedness to Being as such, and it has to be re-newed constantly. But we must at once correct this statement, since it is not up to the freedom of the individual to decide for existence. The decision for existence is rather an affirmative acknowledgement of the fact that we are "thrown" into existence. To take up this "being-thrown" as my own possibility means to decide for existence and to enter into the actual relatedness of Being as such. Whenever Heidegger speaks of "existence," this positive implication must be seen, that Human being has responded to the challenging claim of Pure Being. Existence implies a transcending attitude of Human being, namely to ex-pose one's self to Being as such. Existence is meant as *ex-sistere*, to ex-pose or project one's self into Being. Existence is, to say it as Tillich does: man with "the courage to be in spite of," and to say it with Heidegger: the courage to be in the horizon of Nothingness.

Thus elucidation of Human being is an indispensable presupposition when dealing with a quest of Being as such. Indeed, the philosopher has to begin with the question of himself in order to lay the basis or fundamentals of an existentialist analysis of Human being. He has to begin with a "fundamental ontology."

This fundamental ontology is nothing else than a

phenomenological anthropology. That means Human
being is questioned in regard to its existence, and this is
the very source of ontological interest. In other words,
the quest is to lift the Being reflected by the phenomenon of Human being into the clarity of conscious speaking. This method which is called phenomenology and
was first developed by E. Husserl, intends to lay bare
and to expose that which shows itself within concrete
being.[10]

Heidegger approaches Human being in order to question it about Being as such. Which Human being? The
average Human being must be approached in order to
recognize essential structures valid for all mankind. The
concern is primitive and naive Human being. Just here
the tendency becomes obvious that the self-understanding of the average man is rooted in daily tasks, in that
which is Concrete being, and not Being as such. This
phenomenon is the inference of our human being-in-the-
world. And this our being-in-the-world is the specific
mode of our being here. In order to dis-close Being as
such first of all we must recognize man's being-in-the-
world as his fundamental nature. Man without world
would be a mere fiction, would be a *Homunculus.* World
and man, Human being and this-worldliness are essentially correlated. Thus: to be in the world is a fundamental character of Human being, it reveals the fact of our
being-thrown.[11] But Human being has the possibility of
recognizing this being-thrown into the world and thus of
transcending it, namely by exposing one's self to the
totality of Being as such and by enduring such an ex-
posed or ecstatic existence.[12] Yet this ex-sisting and
self-ex-posing existence does not mean that man with-
draws from the world. World and Human being are in-
separable, as we saw. To exist, to expose one's self means

only, but decisively, something positive. It means that Human being projects itself towards Being as such.

This self-projecting of Human being towards Being is the response to the factuality of our being-thrown here and now into the world. Just because Heidegger knows very well that no Human being has knowledge about its whence and whither, that nobody was ever asked about his desires with regard to existence, that our being-thrown is our human destiny—just for that reason he emphasizes the possibility of transcending this sheer factuality. How can this be done? In exposing ourselves to Being, deciding for our destiny, projecting ourself to that which is ahead.

The ultimate and essential project of Human being is given when man anticipates and acknowledges *death* as the end of Human being.[13] Man is a finite being. Finiteness and worldliness are essential features of his structure. It is in facing *death* that finiteness becomes most clear. Yet the average and standardized man tries to escape the reality of death, to live as if there is no such final end as death. Therefore one does not mention death. One de-realizes its cruel factuality. Funeral homes with their tasteless beautification of death are symptoms, not causes, of this phenomenon of man's being-thrown. The average man constantly searches for narcotics, because death is Nothingness, and Nothingness is the ever-present sword of Damocles, suspended over our Human being by a single hair. However, man cannot escape it just by shutting his eyes. With his fear of death man has only one possibility of existing: he has to appropriate his death by anticipating its futurity and making it a part of his present. This fact—"I must die"—we have to take into our daily life and to live through. When thus anticipating death, we are existing. Doing so we are gaining

"freedom toward death." Heidegger says: "Human
being dies as long as it exists." [14] This does not mean
that each minute of our life we are coming nearer to the
end of life. This would be a banality. However, it means
that as long as we exist, i.e. consciously exist, as parts of
a totality, we are aware of the finiteness of our human
being. We acknowledge our final finiteness and acknowledge Being as such in facing the threat of Nothingness.

What is it that points to death as a constant reality?
It is given by the *anxiety* present in all men, openly or
secretly. Anxiety is something else than fear. Fear is concerned with the particular and definite intramundane
danger. On the other hand, anxiety is concerned with the
whole of our worldly being-there.[15] Anxiety is indefinite and total; it has no concrete object; it is ultimately
concerned with nothing but knows about the monstrous
reality of this Nothingness. Heidegger once said: The
object of anxiety is our "to be in the world." [16] Anxiety
comes from the Latin word *angustia*, i.e. narrowness. It
is a narrowness into which we are squeezed by our being-
thrown into the world. Such anxiety can by no means be
leveled down into a psychological category. It is an ontological category. "Being toward death is essentially anxiety," Heidegger says.[17]

Here in the United States one is used to consider anxiety as a phenomenon of weakness, as a lack of strength
and lack of courage—perhaps even as un-American behavior. What is meant in this criticism is not anxiety but
fear, for instance fear of a radically total war, fear of
the atom or H-bomb, fear of possible but always concrete dangers threatening us. Yet anxiety is something
else. It is expressing our encounter with Being as such
and with Nothingness. "The whole of Being seems to

drift away into nothing." [18] Anxiety is not a negative
reaction but a positive phenomenon since just here
Being as such reveals itself in the horizon of Nothingness. Therefore, anxiety cannot be subdued and cannot
be misinterpreted as cowardliness. On the contrary, anxiety confronting man with Nothingness ex-poses him to
Pure Being so that man truly exists. Being open-minded
to our anxiety, we are able to transcend it. Called to
anticipate the final end into our present we become free
from contingencies and finiteness. Thus Nothingness is a
part of our Human being in its essential relatedness to
Being as such. And to Being as such, i.e. transcendency
in its absolute meaning, nothing is to be compared, but
something is to be related: namely Nothingness. This
relatedness we may even interpret as follows: Nothingness *belongs* to Being as such.[19]

The fact that with Heidegger the concepts of death,
the end, anxiety, Nothingness are obviously of basic importance has nothing to do with nihilism or pessimism.
With these categories so much watered down we cannot
do justice to the radical realism and sincere earnestness
of Heidegger's philosophical intention. Death is, by no
means, that which we call the departure from this life;
it is not decomposition of life as it is with animals. With
them death would mean the biological end, the final
point of a temporal line. We would water down Heidegger's term of its meaning in applying death to a particular occurrence of a natural process. Human being in the
face of the final act (*Sein zum Tode*), Human being in
the face of Nothingness, anxiety towards death and yet
freedom towards death—all this means that we as
Human beings transcend vegetative life and mere vitality and arrive at Being as such. We acknowledge death
as a permanent companion and as a neighbor of life.

The call directed to man is therefore: to be open-
minded to our being exposed to death, acknowledge it as
a positive fact, aim for what Rilke called the ability to
read the word death without negative response.[20] When
we are able to do this, we are existing, i.e. ex-posed to
Being as such.

2. *History and Historicity.* Until now we have re-
stricted our interpretation intentionally to Heidegger's
book, *Being and Time.* From now on—though taking
this book as our starting point—we will include Heidegger's more recent publications. We have just tried to
show that for Heidegger Human being means to be
toward death and that man only exists when acknowl-
edging this fact, when appropriating death and thus
advancing in freedom toward death. It may have been
better, perhaps, not to speak of death in general but of
my death and *our* death, since we can only speak about
death as reality in relation to our own self. And when
doing so, we arrive at an existentialist relatedness, which
becomes particularly obvious and problematic as we now
take up the theme of time and the problem of history as
our history.

Heidegger's point of departure has been Wilhelm
Dilthey.[21] Dilthey had already overcome Historicism in
radicalizing the question of history into a question of
man as the subject of history. This principle Heidegger
is developing further. Already in *Being and Time* he
defines time as the temporariness of Human being and
thus sets aside the question of objective time. Heidegger's thesis is that world history, that is, the general
phenomenon which we call history, can only be approxi-
mately understood when we take our starting point with
man's own history, precisely with man's historicity. Thus
whenever the term "historicity" appears, Human being

in its historical self-understanding is concerned.[22] Where then does the phenomenon of man's historicity become manifest? In man's capacity to bring himself into the whole, i.e. when ex-posing himself to the being-to-death when life is marked by the "goal as such." "Temporariness reveals itself as the actual meaning of our being concerned (care)," says Heidegger. In constantly advancing towards death, being always *vers la mort* and not *pour la mort* we are anticipating future in our present. Now and here the future is arriving and is predominant within the whole complex of time.[23] The future is not merely a vague possibility or the remote horizon but in its concrete relatedness to death, rising out of the future, it is an arriving power characterizing the Here and Now and calling men to decision. In fact, history in its deeper meaning begins only where man makes a decision in facing the arrival of future. History does not mean past time. That would be "vulgar history." The past is that time which is dead, where nothing occurs any more. History, on the other hand, is not merely present—since the present does not occur but happens. It arrives and passes by. However, "history as event is the acting through and suffering through of the present, determined by the future and taking over the past."[24] No doubt compared with the current terminology this is a strange definition. Historiography until now was not primarily concerned with the future as the main question—except in some essays by A. Toynbee or Oswald Spengler. With Heidegger history is derived from historicity. And the concept of historicity which was already defined and introduced by R. G. Collingwood, independently of Heidegger and Jaspers, is taken over by Erich Frank.

In the recent books—long after his work *Being and Time*—Heidegger no longer derives history from the

temporariness of Human being. Now he defines history as sent by Being as such, as the outcome of the
absolute Being which *is* behind all Concrete being and
which sets forth the essential events. Now history has
become destiny, designated to man by Being as such.
In German Heidegger uses *Geschick* instead of *Ge-
schichte.* It is almost impossible to present this specific
terminology of Heidegger's in adequate English terms,
since here, as often with Heidegger, philosophy is essentially connected with philology, i.e. with a penetrating investigation and discrimination of the semantic
rules of German words which Heidegger uses as most appropriate vehicles of his thinking.

Yet, we are arriving at a turning point in Heidegger's
thinking. He himself mentions this turn and dates it
back to the year 1930 when his article "On the Essence
of Truth" was written.[25] In Heidegger's *Introduction into
Metaphysics,* lectures of the year 1935, the turn is obvious. It is not merely a change in terminology, it rather
concerns the content. No more the Being of Human
being bound with time is marking the direction of his
search. But now his ambition is to embrace Being as
such in its totality. Being as such becomes so to say the
deus ex machina of history. The problem of history once
entangled with Human being is now a problem of Being
as such. "To destiny (destined event) comes Pure Being
in manifesting itself," Heidegger says. In other words,
Being as such becomes history in revealing and manifesting itself. Yet, such self-manifestation and self-disclosure
of Being as such within destined events is not identical
with history as the sequences of occurrences, it is not
that ever-changing vulgar world history as we may think
of when using our term "history." But, Being as such
manifesting itself within destined events very rarely

occurs, namely only when the destined event of the truth of Being occurs. Obviously Heidegger means that history occurs where and when man responds to the destiny sent by Being as such. History is therefore nothing else but history of destiny, sent by Being as such and reflected in human decision.[26] This "history of Being" has the twofold meaning that the genitive "of Being" is *genitivus subjectivus*, genitive of authorship, and *genitivus objectivus*, the genitive of content. In other words, the object of history, namely Being, is at the same time operating subject.[27]

Also in Heidegger's latest writings the predominant role is given to the future. He speaks about an eschatology of Being.[28] And in speaking thus about the final revealment of Being, he refers back to the first speaking of the revealment of Being. Now Heidegger often uses the double connotation of a German word. Here he does so with the word "once," *einst*, as a starting point for his thought. *Einst* can mean, then, "once upon a time in the very beginning." But it can also mean "at some day in the very last days." By means of the German word *einst* Heidegger is able to connect primeval history and eschatological occurrences, though in particular this correlation remains unexplained. Heidegger speaks in this context about a parousia of Being as such,[29] but when scrutinizing its meaning, one discovers that it points toward the being present in Being as such, manifest as well in world-night or in world-light as in an eternal night or in an eternal morning. Here the analyst of Human being and existence seems to become a prophet and seer,[30] though not so much concerned with what the future really will bring about as with *how* man reacts to the actual now and here. His criticism of present life is shaped in a project of eschatological possibilities, which are presented with a code-name: eschatology or parousia of Being. That means that the daring project of a history of the future, expressed as eschatology of Being, points toward the historicity of man. It is not meant as a speculation or as an apocalyptic calendar, though it is consciously ambiguous in its setting. Just this ambiguity is meant as a challenge to man in order to provoke his decision as response so that the "epoch-making character of Being as such" comes to pass when human existence exposes itself to ec-stasy.[31] (With ec-stasy Heidegger means obviously the threat *and* bliss of Being and Nothingness.) Such a return of man to ecstasy is the true though hidden history. The eschatology of Being serves Being in bringing historical Human existence into the right direction towards Being as such.

Yet, the ontological seer, though projecting his apocalypse in the form of a question, falls back into the vulgar history of the future when he asks: "Are we the latecomers of an era which soon is approaching its final ending, in a desert of uniform order? . . . or, have we arrived at the eve of tremendous transformations of the globe and of the historical realm to which our globe is fastened? Are we in the very eve of a night which leads towards a new morning? Are we setting out wandering toward the realm where the sun of world's history is setting? Does the land of the eve still lie before us? . . . *Are* we really the latecomers who we are? Or are we at the same time the predecessors of a new age to come, which has left behind all our present concepts of history?"[32]

Heidegger does not answer his questions because the eschatological concern will only unlock man for the destiny of Being, or, as Tillich puts it, "resolve man for resolution." This courage to be, as Tillich says, this openness for the operating Being, as Heidegger puts it, requires questions in order to gain the searching unrest and the necessary insecurity over against the destiny of Being. What Heidegger aims at is therefore not knowledge to be passed on but "truth" as an occurring event. He wants us to be on the way, to be on the track, where to one seemingly lost in the wilderness the anxiety of nothingness is suddenly laid bare, and thus Being as such reveals itself. Speaking about the shepherd as the guardian of Being as such, he says that, "He can only be the shepherd of Being in so far as he remains the guardian of Nothingness. Both are one and the same. Man can only achieve both through resoluteness of his Human being." [33]

Heidegger's concept of history is hard to characterize by qualifying catch words. Maybe this is a point in favor of his project. Heidegger's philosophy is on the one hand strongly opposed to any belief in progress; on the other hand, he rejects pessimistic views of world decline, conceptions of history which infer a movement of decadence. To be sure, he evaluates Western European history as "decline of metaphysics" and as "concealing of Being as such." He says, "Since the religious trinity—Heracles, Dionysos and Christ—have left this world, the eve of the world approaches night." [34] However, this does not indicate that with night the final end is arriving. On the contrary, in the middle of the world-night Being as such suddenly will irradiate, the light of Being will fall in, and thus when the danger is most acute, the destiny of Being and Nothingness will transform night into day, eve into a new morn. And this eschatological event of Being's advent will occur at once together with a transformation of man's essence. We never will be able to pin down a prime cause for this. [35] Here obviously the Christian dialecticism of sin and grace is taken up as a basis for a philosophical-ontological prophecy.

I must break off here in order to take up the last question, the question of whether this existentialism or existential ontology has anything to do with Christianity and Christian faith.

HEIDEGGER AND CHRISTIAN FAITH

The "*philosophical* trinity" of modern existentialism, Martin Heidegger, Karl Jaspers and Jean-Paul Sartre, though all taking human existence as their starting point, widely diverge in their attitude toward Christian faith and the phenomenon of Christianity (as they do in their basic philosophical intention and in their language). Sartre may almost be defined as a fighting atheist, though even in his thinking we find, though perverted, Christian elements and patterns. Jaspers must be characterized as an extreme liberal Protestant who, concerned with Jesus as a type for failing mankind, uses him to support his "philosophical faith." [36] Much more difficult, because more complex, is the investigation of Heidegger's relationship to Christian faith.

He is more familiar than most scholars are with Augustine's writings, with Scholasticism, with Luther. He has studied Sören Kierkegaard extensively. During his five years at Marburg University while writing his basic work, *Being and Time*, he worked with Rudolf Bultmann.[37] Heidegger does not study the sources in translation, nor does he take up monographs with well selected quotations. He is one of those rare philosophers who go *ad fontes* with penetrating zeal, one of those who are thoroughly acquainted with the history of philosophy. In recent years his chief sources were the pre-

Socratic writings and such poets as Hölderlin and Rilke.
Christ Jesus never has been explicitly the impulse of
his philosophical discrimination. Never has he taken up
the New Testament as a starting point for his thinking,
though a New Testament student may feel tempted to
express some of Heidegger's complicated conceptions,
for instance, those about the parousia of Being as such,
in the simple language of the synoptic Jesus.

From all that we have seen up to now there can be no
doubt that Heidegger can easily be used for designing
a phenomenology of religion and can as easily be mis-
used for displaying a psychology of religion. Yet, one
must emphasize that Heidegger in his work *Being and
Time* was much more helpful for Christian theology,
namely by his defined categories, than the Heidegger of
today, who is wandering on the jungle trail and enjoying
his being lost in the woods because there Being as such
reveals itself. In his book *Holzwege* Heidegger is advancing into the realm of religious pathos and ethos. He
speaks about God and gods, about hale and holy, about
evil and modern man's self-affirmation. He speaks of
eschatology and parousia, yet at least in the form of his
terminology he is not too far from Meister Eckhart's
mysticism of Being.

Heidegger's intention to build a bridge over the gap
between transcendence and immanence leads into the
danger of a monism of Being. The impulse for this intention is given by the danger of a dualistic conception
which would break into parts the totality of Being as
such. Yet Heidegger is willing to say: "Man can never
put himself into the place of God because the essence
of his Human being never reaches the realm of God's
Being." [38] This statement reaffirms a gap and excludes
mysticism as an inherent tendency of his thought. In fact,

Heidegger takes up a notion in Kierkegaard's statement about the "infinite qualitative distinction between God and man," but he gives in his own philosophical view a different interpretation to this. For the poetical language such as Heidegger uses in his *Holzwege* endangers Christian theology because of its vague and indefinite connotations, while the phenomenological terminology in *Being and Time* was helpful in its penetrating discrimination.

With emphasis we must say that Heidegger is not an atheist at all. He is a religious thinker as long as we understand "religion" in its deeper meaning as relatedness to God, although we cannot assert that the God in whom the Christian faith believes, God as a person and not as a neutral concept of Being as such, is the god of Heidegger. Yet we should recognize that Heidegger ultimately is concerned in the re-establishment of relatedness between man and the transcendental Being in order to expose man to the totality of Being. We cannot overlook that with Heidegger Being as such is essentially Transcendency as such. When Heidegger criticizes man as enslaved by the pseudo-security of concrete objects, by the demon of space and technique, when he demasks man in his almost pathological self-affirmation, when he analyzes idle talk and gossip as an attempt to escape from ultimate anxiety towards death—then he says nothing else than what Paul has said characterizing man according to the flesh. In fact Heidegger's portrait of the thrown and fallen man is very similar to what Paul with the Greek term καυχᾶσθαι says about self-glorification and boasting. And the same can be said about Heidegger's term "world" which in its structure is more Pauline than Greek, since in Greek philosophy cosmos means the ordered world as a totality, the world as a piece of art.

With Paul cosmos means the human world as this-worldiness rendered into a power by man himself. Like Paul, Heidegger emphasizes the close relatedness of world to man and of man to world, yet without theological accentuation. For Paul world implies sin, while for Heidegger it is a neutral phenomenon, somehow representative of Concrete Being.

From Heidegger's thought we can never deduce a theological doctrine. Neither does one see how man's self-affirmation and being-thrown are related to evil. In his letter on Humanism Heidegger says that "the evil appears together with the Holy in the radiance of Being as such." [39] For our question this statement has a twofold significance. On the one side it repeats the New Testament statement to the effect that sin and evil can only be recognized on the basis of faith and grace. Here the dialecticism of Christian theology again becomes obvious. On the other hand, the evil does not consist in the mere badness of man, but it originates from evil or wrath or ire. The evil is not a lack of Being, nor is it a nothing in the sense of Neo-platonism. It is not an anthropological category since the initiator of evil is a power beyond man. Evil may be interpreted as the active nihilation which is coming from Being as well as from Nothingness. From this it can be inferred that Heidegger considers man as a being bound by a destination destined from outside, from beyond, and that man's decision is finally no more than an affirmation, affirmative or negative response to this call from beyond, to this challenging Being as such, or Nothingness. As a New Testament student I cannot refrain from saying that it is just this interrelation and correlation of freedom *and* predestination explained by Paul in his letter to the Romans, Chapters 9 to 11, which we rediscover here in philosophical terms. Perhaps it is more in the line of Heidegger when we quote Paul's word in Philippians 2:12 f: "Work out your own salvation with fear and trembling, for God is at work in you, both to will and to work for his good pleasure." Yet Heidegger would render this soteriological idea into an ontological one and put it perhaps like this: Decide yourself for Being as such in spite of all your anxiety concerning Nothingness, since Being as such leads you through its destiny into the light of Being and into the freedom towards death.

What the New Testament says about life as ζωή in contrast to βίος Heidegger expresses by Being as such in contrast to Concrete being. Yet, these are only analogous but not identical conceptions. These are not identical conceptions because the New Testament antithesis to life (as ζωή) is death (θάνατος), and this is understood as remoteness from God. But the decisive point in the New Testament is this, that death has lost its power in spite of man's biological end wherever man in faith and through grace participates in the true life, which can be given already in this world where we are in faith and in hope. For Paul and John death as power is overcome. "Death is swallowed up in victory" (I Cor. 15:54). Here no longer dominates the annihilating Nothingness; here physical death is only a door, a passage, which refers only to the flesh "of Human being," but does not affect any more the pneumatic spiritual existence. To use Heidegger's terminology we must say: the Christian sees that death is disarmed, death affects only Concrete being but no more the Pure Being of our existence. Decisively different is death in Heidegger's philosophy: here death never means the threshold between two scenes or between two eons, understood as the transcendent and immanent realms. Neither is death—as with Jaspers—

the heroic failure of human existence. Such conceptions do belittle the reality of death and do interpret death as a biological occurrence. For Heidegger death is the destiny of Being and the final borderline which can *never* be transcended. But with death the advent or parousia of Being occurs. The revealed truth opens up, so that Heidegger can even speak about the "mercy of death." Heidegger never speaks about Being after death. For him the eschatology of Being is fulfilled and closed with the decisive parousia of Being as such coming together in and with death.

When studying Heidegger and when thinking together with him, one cannot avoid the question: do not his conceptions of Being and of Nothingness finally present two aspects of one and the same absolute Being?

As far as I can see, Heidegger's analysis of Human existence more than any other modern philosophy offers structures and defines terms fit for theologically clear speaking. This does not mean that he built up some vestibule for systematic theology. Neither do I think that he should have a monument in the Propylaea of a theological Acropolis. What I want to say is this: Heidegger formulates anew and radicalizes the question of man for the meaning of Being as such, which had been lost or belittled for ages. He lays bare modern escapism into all sorts of pseudo-security and sets in motion thinking as the quest and aim for genuine learning. More than that, he offers categories which enable us as Christian theologians to lift up the knowledge inherent in faith into the clarity of a defined language. His linguistic creativeness in spite of its archaic arbitrariness makes language again a genuine confession of our existence.

Until now we have pointed out what is implicit in Heidegger's writings. What now about his explicit relationship to Christianity? Let me quote and translate a passage from his last book, *Introduction into Metaphysics*: "He, to whom the Bible is the divine revelation and the truth, has already the answer when concerned with the question, Why is there anything at all and not rather nothing? His answer is: God is the uncreated creator of concrete being. Though one at home in such faith may be able to follow our question to a certain degree, he cannot really start such a quest without giving up himself as a faithful believer with all the consequences of such a stand. He can only behave as if . . . Yet on the other hand, belief, not permanently exposing itself to the question and danger of unbelief, is no faith at all, but mere convenience, and agreement with one's self to keep the doctrine as to a comforting tradition. That is neither faith nor quest but indifference, a capacity for handling everything without commitment but with much interest, be it faith or quest." [40] What Heidegger says in this statement is primarily that a Fundamentalist can neither be a philosopher nor arrive at ultimate questions. Nor is he able to question his own self, because to him the Bible is a compendium of answers to all questions about the absolute and concrete Being. I think Heidegger is right. Such Fundamentalist belief is no faith because here for the sake of self-security venturing self-surrender as an essential feature of faith is eliminated. Thus doubt and unbelief are never encountered but are suppressed. In fact it is this quotation which shows Heidegger's deeper understanding of faith as given in the New Testament especially in Paul and proves Heidegger's deep *inter-esse* with Christian faith. Heidegger's criticism refers only to those cases where "belief does not expose itself to the question and danger of unbelief," namely when faith is misunderstood as acknowledgement of doctrines. In other words, Heidegger's ontological verdict is directed against *fides quae creditur* only and not against the Protestant-Pauline *fides qua creditur.*

That Heidegger does not criticize faith as such but only the misunderstood faith as consent to churchly tradition may be proved by another passage. "It is only in periods which no more believe in the true and great task of theology that the fatal opinion comes up that one should support or substitute theology with philosophy in order to meet the general tendencies of today's culture." [41] Such criticism of a propagandistic or even apologetic misuse of philosophy is all right. We do not need philosophical façades. But on the other hand, we cannot overlook the fact that philosophy and theology have at least one topic in common: man's being in the midst of this world. At this point both disciplines may and, to a large extent, must use one and the same vocabulary, the vocabulary of their time, without being blamed for pragmatic, modernizing tendencies. Furthermore, we cannot overlook the fact that no philosopher can cast off the historical tradition of theology any more than a theologian (not even a pietistic Biblicist) can withdraw entirely from the philosophical tradition and contemporary philosophical concepts. Language is, to use Heidegger's own words, a temple of Being, an architecture of actual thinking. What has been alive in the action of thinking is rendered into static terms in Language. Neutralizing and individualizing language always involves the venturesome attitude.

When reading Heidegger critically one cannot but think that he strongly criticizes empirical Christendom, ecclesiastical Christianity of all denominations. In the course of his interpretation of Nietzsche he writes: "The churchly world has become lifeless, dead. Well, here and there one shall find faith in Christ. But love, ruling in this world, is no more the operating, effective principle of what now is going on. The transcendent ground of the transcendent world, thought as the creative reality of everything which is real, has become unreal. Such is the metaphysical meaning of Nietzsche's word 'God is dead'." [42]

This statement, however questionable it may be in its phrasing, is more a criticism of our pseudo-Christian culture than of Christianity itself. In another place Heidegger derives even the active atheism of our time from our empirical Christianity, that is from empirical church life. [43] This is a very serious criticism, and one should not throw it away too early. Yet even here Heidegger's criticism is based not upon a negation of faith in Christ but upon a deeper insight into the New Testament Kerygma. To him the active atheism of our age is given by the twofold process of Christianizing a world-view (*Weltanschauung*) and of perverting Christianity into a world-view and conception of the universe. In other words, Heidegger criticizes the fact that the stumbling block of the Christian message, man's redemption through and in Christ, is objectified, is rendered into a pseudo-objective dogma and has thus lost its character as a challenging proclamation and call. What Heidegger really attacks is not Christianity but its transformation or transmutation of "the scandal of the Cross" into a doctrine of principles. That means according to Heidegger a falsification of Being as such into Concrete being. That means that our being on the way as long as we are living in this world is rendered into an ideology of security. It means that we dismiss the basic daring character of faith as adventure and that we finally dismiss the very goal of *faith.* We could also interpret Heidegger as saying that modern Christendom has rendered God and Christ into objects, which can be looked at by beholders without existential commitment and participation, that mankind of today is no more challenged by God and Christ as ruling, blessing and therefore also sometimes punishing subjects who are looking for sub-jects, who want citizens of Jerusalem and not just voters choosing according to the advantage of their own this-worldly realm.

While we have some doubts about Heidegger in his recent publications, especially about what he says in *Holzwege* concerning his being in the neighborhood of Being and of God's advent, we must face the fact that his criticism of empirical Christianity has some truth in it. Heidegger criticizes a misunderstanding of Christianity as a result, over against a Christianity which should be the constant attempt and the constant goal. Heidegger knows about the Christian dialecticism of being as a way of becoming. On the other side, we must criticize the Heidegger of today as a thinker who tries to become a poet. We must criticize him as a philosopher who is pretending to be a super-theologian. His language has become too much of an archaic temple [44] where speaking originates from the "dictating of Being as such." [45] Then the speaking of the philosopher becomes a reflex or an echo of a verbal inspiration coming from Being. Here philosophy is transcending itself in pretending to be a "revelation" of the "unhidden truth." In these recent publications Heidegger demands that reason has to be dismissed in order to enable the thinking of Being as such. And here thinking means to have an ear which listening, perceives. Such listening and perceiving thought seems to be identical with faith, leaving far behind all logicism, because here Being as such reveals itself. [46]

It is very hard, indeed, to enter a dialogue with the Heidegger of recent years, since reason and logicism are indispensable for any sort of dialogue and discussion. When thought is interpreted as listening to the dictating Being as such, it becomes inspiration. It is made into an authority, reasonable thinking is dismissed, and a fundamentalistic philosophy is established.

Yet, I will not conclude with such criticisms. Since taking into account as a Christian theologian what Heidegger has set forth in books and lectures up to now, gratitude prevails and not objection. Certainly we cannot characterize Heidegger as an outspoken Christian existentialist, since "Christian" means that man confesses his relatedness to Christ in faith. As Heidegger has never made such confessions, we should be cautious with these qualifications. Neither the fact that he nowhere has said anything against genuine Christian faith nor his implicit statements about the phenomenon of Christian faith suffices to characterize him as a Christian existentialist. In fact, I have no doubts that Heidegger does not want to be characterized by these terms. On the other hand it would be a mistake to put Heidegger into an antithesis to Christian faith. Sincere faith is not a phenomenon of Concrete being and the flexibility of Heidegger's thoughtful language presents many possibilities for interpretation. Judgment about what remains unsaid with Heidegger is left to God and not to man's jurisdiction.

Heidegger's significance for Western culture—and that means also for Christian culture in its wider sense—lies in the fact that he puts anew and radically before us the basic question of metaphysics, namely, why is there anything at all and not rather nothing? We may perhaps say that the special mission of Heidegger's thinking lies in the fact that he has rediscovered the creative tension between Greek and Christian thinking and that for him truth can be elucidated only by human existence being on the way. Especially in this concept that human being is existing only as long as it recognizes itself as being on the way—not knowing all the solutions of our riddles concerning the universe and its history, not having obtained salvation, not having reached the goal—just here the pre-Socratic and the earliest Christian thinking have a common ground. We as Christian theologians can only appreciate that a philosopher of the rank of Heidegger recognizes as the task of thinking first of all the exposition of existential questions, namely, putting questions into the right frame, defining our own problems, recognizing and rediscovering the very facts of our own Human being.

It seems to me important that when Heidegger gives an existentialist analysis of Human being, namely of natural man before his decision for faith in Christ, he obviously is himself marked by the Christian tradition. Man as such, stamped by guilt, fear, anxiety, by his being-thrown-into-the-world, all this in its terminology and in its intention is evidently influenced by a Christian viewpoint. Furthermore, Heidegger has outlined a conception of history in which all occurrences are related to or epitomized by man's historicity. It is here that Heidegger has developed a concept in his own philosophy which is based upon a Christian conception. Heidegger thus finally overcomes the "idea of history" current since Descartes, which constituted a cleavage between the searching subject and the searched-for object and which had become a general hypothesis of scholarly research in our modern times. Perhaps subconsciously more than consciously Heidegger gives us back a purified Christian heritage which had been lost for ages.

Two critical problems of our present theological discussion are decisively influenced by Heidegger. The first is the question about the truth of Christian eschatology, and the second, the discussions about the problem of hermeneutics. Both problems go back to the distinction which Heidegger first introduced, the distinction between the history of facts and the historicity of man.

The obvious significance of Heidegger for Christian theology lies in his unfolding and defining of categories. Three Protestant theologians of outstanding rank have taken up Heidegger's questions and his analysis of concepts: on the one side Paul Tillich influenced by Heidegger's ontology, and on the other side Rudolf Bultmann as a New Testament scholar and Friedrich Gogarten as a systematic theologian, both influenced more by his hermeneutical principles. All three are indebted to Heidegger's concept of existence and by his concept of the historicity of man. One cannot say that they have taken over the philosophical *results* of Heidegger, but one must say that they have taken up his questions, used them in a legitimate way and that they have set in motion the thinking of our time. If we agree that Christian theology means to speak about existential faith in existentialist terms, we urgently need defined terms. Language is the vehicle of thought and not an escape into mystical ambiguity. Heidegger, the thinker of *Being and Time,* is at least a companion of and helper for a theologian who aims to make the truth of faith speak in the midst of this world, this world of Concrete Being. Thus Heidegger is opening up new possibilities of hearing and understanding. Heidegger's significance for philosophy lies in his existentialist ontology. His importance for theology lies in his categories and in his hermeneutical impulses.

7. *Existentialist Aspects of Modern Art*

To do justice to my subject I should really write three books—one on existentialism, one on art, and one on religion. Then I should relate these three to each other. Here, however, all this has to be done in the narrow space of a single chapter.

MEANING AND HISTORY OF EXISTENTIALISM

Let me start with the first "book." First, I want to devote a few words to what I believe existentialism is, just as the other contributors to this volume have given some description or definition of what they understand by existentialism. I distinguish three meanings of this term:

128

1. RAPHAEL *The Alba Madonna*

Courtesy the National Gallery of Art, Washington, D. C., Mellon Collection

Owned by the artist. Photo courtesy the Museum of Modern Art, New York

2. PABLO PICASSO *Guernica*

3. VINCENT VAN GOGH   *Starry Night*

4. RUBENS *Landscape with an Avenue of Trees*

5. GEORGES ROUAULT *Miserere*

Plate 46 from the series: *The just, like sandalwood, perfume the ax that strikes them.*

6. MATHIAS GRÜNEWALD *Crucifixion*

Detail of the figure of Christ.

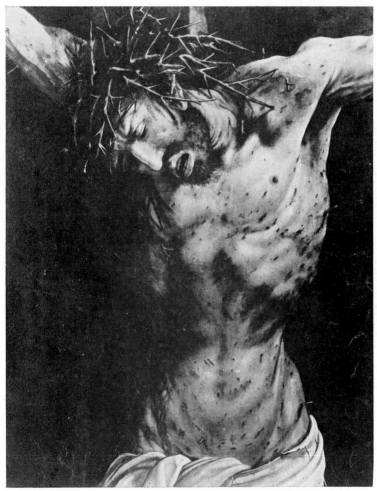

Courtesy the Colmar Museum, France

7. GIORGIO DE CHIRICO   *Toys of a Prince*

existentialism as an element in all important human thinking, existentialism as a revolt against some features of the industrial society of the nineteenth century, and existentialism as a mirror of the situation of sensitive human beings in our twentieth century. Of course the main emphasis will be on the last meaning of this term. I believe that most creative art, literature and philosophy in the twentieth century is in its very essence existentialist. And this is the reason why I have proposed to address myself to existentialist elements in recent visual art. I believe that the people for whom visual impressions are important will perhaps understand what existentialism means better by looking at modern art than by reading recent philosophers.

Existentialism as a universal element in all thinking is the attempt of man to describe his existence and its conflicts, the origin of these conflicts, and the anticipations of overcoming them. In this sense, the first classical philosopher who had many existentialist elements in his thinking was Plato. I refer here especially to those instances where he employs mythology, for existence, in distinction from essence (from what man essentially is), cannot be derived in terms of necessity from his essential nature. Existence is that which stands against essence although it is dependent on essence. Plato uses existentialist terms when he speaks of the transition from existence to essence or from essence to existence; when he speaks of the fall of the souls; when he speaks of the seeming but not true character of the world of appearances and opinions; or when he speaks of the bondage of the soul in the cave of shadows. In many other cases he brings into his philosophy existentialist elements, and he is wise enough to know that this cannot be done in terms of essentialist analysis.

There are existentialist elements in early Christian
theology—very outspoken elements for instance in Augustine and his doctrine of man's estrangement from his
true essence, from his union with God as his creative
ground. There are existentialist elements in classical
theology, in the Middle Ages, and in Protestantism.
Wherever man's predicament is described either theologically or philosophically, either poetically or artisti-
cally, there we have existentialist elements. This is the
first meaning of this word.

The second meaning is existentialism as a revolt. It is
a revolt which started almost at the moment when
modern industrial society found its fundamental concepts, in the seventeenth century. The man who first expressed these elements as a revolt was Pascal, although
at the same time he made great contributions to the development of modern thinking by his mathematical
discoveries. From Pascal on, we have had an uninter-
rupted series of men who repeated this protest against
the attitude of industrial society. Man was considered
to be only a part, an element in the great machine of the
Newtonian World, and, later on, an element in the great
social process of production and consumption in which
we all are now living. The protest against this view was
a protest of the existing man, of man in his estrangement,
his finitude, in his feeling of guilt and meaninglessness.
It was a protest against the world view in which man
is nothing but a piece of an all-embracing mechanical
reality, be it in physical terms, be it in economic or
sociological terms, or even be it in psychological terms.
This protest was continued in the nineteenth century by
the founders of existentialism (in the special sense of the
word) Schelling, in his old age, realized that he had to
protest not only against his former pupil and friend,

Hegel, but also against the Schelling of his earlier years, and introduced most of the categories in which present day existentialism is thinking. From him, people like Kierkegaard, Engels, and Feuerbach took concepts of anti-essentialist philosophy. These protesting men— Kierkegaard, Marx, Feuerbach, Trendelenburg, later Nietzsche, and at the end of the century people like Bergson and Whitehead—these are people who wanted to save human existence from being swallowed by the essential structure of industrial society in which man was in danger of becoming a thing.

With the beginning of the twentieth century this feeling became much more universal. The people whom I have just cited were lonely prophets, often in despair, often at the boundary line of insanity in their desperate and futile fight against the over-powering forms of modern industrial society. In the twentieth century the outcry of existentialism became universal. It became the subject matter of some great philosophers, such as Heidegger, Jaspers, Sartre, Marcel, and many others; it became a topic of the drama; it became effective in poetry. After some predecessors like Beaudelaire and Rimbaud in the nineteenth century it has become widespread, and men like Eliot and Auden are widely known. It was expressed especially powerfully in the novel. In two of Kafka's main novels, *The Castle* and *The Trial,* we have descriptions of the two fundamental anxieties. The anxiety of meaninglessness is described in *The Castle.* He himself, Mr. K., tries in vain to reach the sources of meaning which direct all life in the village in which he lives, and he never reaches them. The anxiety of guilt is described in *The Trial,* where guilt is an objective factor. The protagonist does not know why he is accused, or who accuses him, he only knows he is accused. He is on trial, he cannot do anything against it, and finally the guilt overcomes him and brings him to judgment and death.

I believe that developments similar to these have taken place in the realm of art. And out of the different visual arts I want to take, not on principle, but for reasons of expediency, painting alone. Painting will reveal some of the innermost motives of existentialism if we are able to analyze the creations since the turn of the century in the right way. In order to do this I want to go immediately to the second "book" and say a few words about religion and about the relationship of religion and art.

LEVELS OF RELATION BETWEEN RELIGION AND ART

Religion means being ultimately concerned, asking the question of "to be or not to be" with respect to the meaning of one's existence, and having symbols in which this question is answered. This is the largest and most basic concept of religion. And the whole development, not only of modern art but also of existentialism in all its realms—and that means of the culture of the twentieth century—is only possible if we understand that this is fundamentally what religion means: being ultimately concerned about one's own being, about one's self and one's world, about its meaning and its estrangement and its finitude. If this is religion, we must distinguish from it religion in a narrower sense, namely, religion as having a set of symbols, normally of divine beings or a divine being, having symbolic statements about activities of these gods or this god, having ritual activities and doctrinal formulations about their relationship to us. This is religion in the narrower sense, where religion is identified first of all as a belief in the existence of a God, and then with intellectual and practical activities following out of this belief. When we speak about religion and art, we must speak in terms of both concepts.

When we hear the words, "religious art," we usually believe that one refers to particular religious symbols like pictures of Christ, pictures of the Holy Virgin and Child, pictures of Saints and their stories, and many other religious symbols. Now this is one meaning of religious art; but there is another following from the larger concept of religion, namely, art as an expression of an ultimate concern. Naturally, it will be an esthetic expression, an artistic expression, but it will be an expression of ultimate concern. And if we distinguish these two ways in which art can express religion, and religion can appear in art, then it is perhaps expedient to distinguish four levels of the relation of religion and art.

The first level is a style in which ultimate concern is not directly but only indirectly expressed. It is what we usually call secular art, and it has no religious content. It does not deal with the religious symbols and rites of any special religion. This first level deals with landscapes, with human scenes, with portraits, with events, with all kinds of things on the level of secular human existence.

Neither on the second level do we have religious contents—pictures of saints, or of Christ, or of the Holy Virgin. There are no sacred scenes, but there is a style, and the style is the form which expresses the meaning of the period. If you want to know what is the ultimate self-interpretation of an historical period, you must ask, "What kind of style is present in the artistic creations of this period." Style is the over-all form which, in the particular forms of every particular artist and of every

particular school, is still visible as the over-all form;
and this over-all form is the expression of that which unconsciously is present in this period as its self-interpretation, as the answer to the question of the ultimate meaning of its existence. Now the characteristic of this style is
that there is something always breaking through out of
the depths to the surface. Wherever this happens we
have a style that is religious even if there is no religious
content whatsoever depicted. I will come back to this
again since it will be the center of our consideration.
But first let me proceed to the third level.

The third level is the level of secular forms of non-
religious style which nevertheless deals with religious
content. These are pictures of Christ, pictures of the
saints, of the Holy Virgin and the Holy Child. When we
think of this third realm we immediately think of the
art of the High Renaissance. It is a non-religious style
dealing with religious content.

The fourth level is mainly the level on which religious
style and religious content are united. That is an art
which, in the most concrete sense, can be called religious
art. It can be used for liturgical purposes or for private
devotion. In it style and content agree. However, I must
conclude this description of the fourth level with the
question, "Is such a religious art possible today?" And
with this qustion I return to the four levels and call to
your attention a few examples.

1. *Non-religious Style, Non-religious Content.* For the
first level I could cite two examples. The first is a picture
by Jan Steen, "The World Upside Down." I recall
another picture, very similar to this one. It also is
an interior, with play, dance, drunkenness, love, and
everything together—very dynamic, very vital, as was
the old Dutch way at that time. I saw that picture in the

National Gallery, two or three years ago, when I first
started to think about a study on religion and art. I had
wanted to look at religious pictures or at least the pictures where religious style is visible. But it so happened
that I could not look away from that picture very similar to this one by Steen. I asked myself, "What does this
picture express in terms of an ultimate interpretation of
human existence?" And my answer was, "It too expresses
power of being in terms of an unrestricted vitality in
which the self-affirmation of life becomes almost ecstatic." Now one may say that this has nothing to do
with religion. I cannot accept this. I may accept that it
is only indirectly religious. It has neither a religious
style, nor a completely secular style, nor has it any religious content. Nevertheless—and this is a Protestant
principle—God is present in secular existence as much
as he is present in sacred existence. There is no greater
nearness to Him in the one than in the other, and using
this as a yardstick for understanding pictures like this, I
would say that this is the first level of the relation of
religion and art, namely that level in which, in secular
style and without religious content, power of being is
visible, not directly, but indirectly. There is another example, a picture by Rubens with animals and landscape,
"Return of the Prodigal." The landscapes of Rubens, for
some mystical reasons, have always interested me philosophically. (Fig. 4). What is the matter with them? You
are in them somehow, they take you in, you live in them,
they give you a feeling for the cosmos in a rather dynamic
way, though completely on the surface of colors and
forms. There is something in this landscape which you
never would see without the painter, and that is what art
has to do, anyway. Here another entire volume could
start: namely, to show in symbols, taken from ordinary

experience, a level of reality which cannot be grasped in any other way. If this were not the case, art would be unnecessary from the very beginning and should be abolished. But art is necessary. It is as necessary as knowledge and other forms of human spiritual life. It is necessary for it reveals levels of reality, even in such secular objects which are, neither in style nor in content, religious.

2. *Religious Style, Non-religious Content: The Existentialist Level.* I come now to the second level, and this level is the existentialist level. The movement of modern existentialism in visual art starts with Cézanne in France. Let me relate one experience I had two years ago when I was in Paris. There was an exhibit of still lifes, starting with works from the sixteenth and seventeenth century and continuing through to the present day. Progressing in chronological order I noticed a strong trend towards the still life. In some way it became apparent that most modern art has transformed all of reality into forms of still life. What does this mean? It means that organic forms have disappeared, and with them has disappeared idealism which always is connected with the description of the organic forms. The forms of our existence are no more organic. They are atomistic, disrupted. These disrupted forms of our existence are taken by themselves by modern artists as the real elements of reality, and now these artists do a tremendous job with them. They reduce the colorful world of the impressionists and of the beautifying idealists of the past to more and more cubic forms. This treatment begins with Cézanne. Cubic forms are the unorganic forms out of which the world is constituted. But the artists do not accept the statement that these forms are only unorganic. Embodied in this very unorganic form is the power of being itself. In this way

the disruptedness of expressionism, surrealism, and all
the other recent forms of styles, such as cubism and
futurism, is nothing else than an attempt to look into the
depths of reality, below any surface and any beautification of the surface and any organic unity. It is the
attempt to see the elements of reality as fundamental powers of being out of which reality is constructed.

Or, consider another artist, Van Gogh, and, for instance, his "Starry Night" (Fig. 3). Here again we have
the character of going below the surface. It is a description of the creative powers of nature. It goes into the
depths of reality where the forms are dynamically created. He does not accept the surface alone. Therefore he
goes into those depths in which the tension of the forces
creates nature. The same is expressed from the point of
view of human society in Van Gogh's "Night Café." Here
you see something I call late emptiness—only one figure.
The waiter has left, and just one man is sitting there, and
that is all. He represents, in all the beautiful colors you
see, the horror of emptiness.

The Norwegian Munch could be added here. He has
painted pictures not so much of emptiness—although
this factor is also in them, but of horror, crime, shock,
that which is uncanny, that which you cannot grasp. In
this way, this Nordic man also became one of the existentialists, at the same time in which Strindberg wrote
his great existentialist dramas with all the terrible ten-
sions, sufferings, and anxieties.

Then there is Picasso. One of Picasso's most important
pictures bears the title, "Guernica" (Fig. 2). Guernica
was a place in Northern Spain where the Fascist countries, Germany and Italy, helped the Fascist Spaniards
to overthrow the Loyalist government, the official government, because it was leftist. This place, Guernica, a

small town in the country of the Basques, was completely destroyed by a combined air attack by the Italians and Germans. It was the first exercise of what is called, "saturation bombing," a terrible word. That means bombing in such a way that nothing is left. Now Picasso has painted this immense horror—the pieces of reality, men and animals and unorganic pieces of houses all together —in a way in which the "piece" character of our reality is perhaps more horribly visible than in any other of the modern pictures. During one of my lectures I once was asked, "What would you think is the best present-day Protestant religious picture?" I answered almost without hesitating, "Guernica." I named this picture, because it shows the human situation without any cover. It shows what very soon followed in most European countries in terms of the second World War, and it shows what is now in the souls of many Americans as disruptiveness, existential doubt, emptiness and meaninglessness. And if Protestantism means that, first of all, we do not have to cover up anything, but have to look at the human situation in its depths of estrangement and despair, then this is one of the most powerful religious pictures. And, although it has no religious content, it does have religious style in a very deep and profound sense.

Now I come to a man named Braque in France who, in his style, is one of Picasso's followers. The picture to which I wish to refer has the name, "Table." Here you have the dissolution of the organic realities which we usually think of when we speak of a table with things on top of it. Everything is dissolved into planes, lines and colors, elements of reality, but not reality itself. We call this "cubism"; this term naturally demands an explanation. It means that the essence of reality is contained in these original forms. What modern art tries to do is to move away from the surface which had nothing to say any more to men of the twentieth century, and to move to the *Urelemente,* the original elements of reality which in the physical realm are cubes, planes, colors, lines and shadows. From this point of view, such a picture can have a tremendous religious power, and I want to say a few words about this later.

In Germany towards the end of the nineteenth century, and in America with the building of Riverside Church in New York, many pictures were produced by two men, Oude and Hoffman. These pictures all portray Jesus either in terms of a sentimental, religious man, as does the Hoffman work in Riverside Church, or in terms of a rheumatic or otherwise sick, dull school teacher walking through little villages. Now, this kind of picture was supposed to be very religious at that time. I would say that for me, however, religious art must show something of God and the basic structures out of which He has made His reality, and not these sentimentalisms. This, of course, does not exclude occasional romantic expressions within these genuine forms.

As another illustration of the second level I refer to Chagall's picture, "River without Edges." Here again we have nothing which can be understood from the naturalistic point of view. It is strongly symbolistic, and perhaps this is the limit of the picture. However, everybody feels here the metaphysics of time in the wild moving clock and the animal above it and the whole constellation of colors and forms. Here the artist tries to use some elements of the encountered world in order to go beyond the surface into the depths of the phenomenon of time. Time is a river without edges.

Or, take another picture by Chagall, named "Lovers."

Notice how the fantastic element comes in, how the forms are taken out of the possibility of natural relationships. The lover comes from the clouds because he is probably in her imagination much more than in her reality.

Then there is a surrealist, Chirico. One of his pictures is called "Toys of a Prince" (Fig. 7). It is characteristic for existentialist art. I would even say it is surrealistic. What does surrealistic mean? It means the elements of reality are brought into a context which has nothing to do with reality. Surrealism points to special dimensions and qualities of the reality as we encounter it. In some of Chirico's pictures it is infinite space into which we look or it is the loneliness, or the blinding power of the sun; or it is the occasional coming together of elements of reality which have nothing whatsoever to do with each other.

Let me deal now a little bit more systematically with this whole second realm which is the center of our interest. I would call this, in the sense of my basic definition, religious style, although I have alluded to no picture whatsoever which had a religious content. And why is it a religious style? Because it puts the religious question radically, and has the power, the courage, to face the situation out of which this question comes, namely the human predicament. In earlier centuries we have painters who did very similar things. We have it in the mannerist period, after Michelangelo. We have it in some of the Baroque pictures. We find it in people like Goya. We have it in those great demonic pictures by Brueghel and Bosch where elements of the psychological as well as the natural reality are brought into the picture without a naturalistic connection with each other, without a system of categories into which they are put. This is the all-important element in existentialism. The essential categories, time, space, causality, substance, have lost their ultimate power. They give meaning to our world. With their help we can understand things. We can understand that one thing follows the other, one causes the other, one is distinguished from the other, each has its space and its time and so on. But all this no longer applies. Mankind does not feel at home in this world any more. The categories have lost their embracing and overwhelming and asserting power. There is no safety in the world.

We have Psalms in this spirit in the Old Testament, especially in the Book of Job, where it is said of man, "and his place does not know him anymore," and this is repeated in the 90th Psalm. Those are very profound words. The things in these pictures are displaced. Displaced persons are a symbol of our time, and displaced souls can be found in all countries. This large scale displacement of our existence is expressed in these pictures. All this is no positive answer to the question of our existence, and therefore I would agree that there is no Christian existentialism. There are many Christian existentialists; but insofar as they are existentialists they ask the question, show the estrangement, show the finitude, show the meaninglessness. Insofar as they are Christian, they answer these questions as Christians, but not as existentialists. For this reason, I do not believe that the ordinary distinction between atheistic and theistic existentialism makes any sense. As long as an existentialist is theistic he is either not existentialist or he is not really theistic. As far as people like Jaspers, like Kierkegaard, like Heidegger in his last mystical period, like Marcel, are Christians, or at least religious, or at least mystics, they are not existentialists but they answer their own existentialism, and that must be clearly distinguished. Existentialism describes the human situation, and as such it is a decisive element in present day religious thinking and Christian theology.

3. *Non-religious Style, Religious Content.* Now, before coming back to this, I wish to indicate a few examples of the two other levels for a complete picture of the whole situation. A picture which is extremely beautiful, which has a religious subject, is a Raphael Madonna and Child (Fig. 1). It is religious neither in substance nor in style. This is one difference between the Raphael and the Chirico picture. In the Chirico, the disruptiveness of reality is visible; in the Raphael, we have a harmonious humanity which of course is indirectly religious, but is not religious in style. Or take another picture, a Madonna by the French painter Fouquet. The Madonna is a court lady of not too good a reputation. You know who she was, yet she is depicted as a Madonna. That shows that here the religious symbol in the Madonna and Child is not combined with the religious style but is reduced to the mother-child relationship of a great lady of the court of France. Or consider another, a Rubens "Madonna and Child." Here is another type of beautiful lady and another type of child. It is wonderful to look at, but nobody would think that this is the mother of God in the Catholic symbolism of this relationship. This is enough to show that religious content in itself does not give a religious picture, and many of those pictures which you find in the magazines of the churches, in the little Sunday papers in the churches themselves or, even worse, in the assembly rooms of the churches or the offices of the ministers are of this same character. They have religious content but no religious style. In this sense they are dangerously irreligious, and they are something

against which everybody who understands the situation
of our time has to fight.

4. *Religious Style, Religious Content.* Now I come to
the fourth level, namely, pictures in which the religious
form is combined with the religious content. This form
is generally called expressionistic, because it is a form
in which the surface is disrupted in order to express
something. I have already stated that there have been
such pictures long before modern times. Take, for instance, Greco's "Crucifixion." Here you have an absolutely unnatural form of the body. It is an expression of
the esthetic form of the counter-reformation in which a
small tenuous line goes up in ecstatic self-elevation towards the Divine with asceticism and often self-destruction. Or, an even earlier picture of the late gothic period, Mathias Grünewald's famous "Crucifixion" (Fig.
6) on the Isenheim Altar. I believe it is the greatest German picture ever painted, and it shows you that expressionism is by no means a modern invention.

Then there is a modern "Crucifixion" by Sutherland.
There you have very similar expression but in modern forms. This is a recent expressionism using forms
similar to Grünewald's, but with all the elements of
disrupted style which modern art has created. In this
context I put a question which I cannot answer: Is it
possible to have this fourth level today? Is it possible to
use these elements of expressionist visual art in dealing
with the traditional symbols of Christianity? Sometimes,
as for instance in the work by Sutherland, I am willing
to say that it is possible. Sometimes I am not willing to
say so.

Nolde, an expressionist of the German school which
started in 1905, like other German expressionists tried to
renew, by means of the expressionistic forms which they

had created, the religious symbols of the past. Sometimes I am impressed by them—but in most cases I feel that they did not succeed. To illustrate this I refer you to Rouault's works, "Christ mocked by the soldiers," and plate 46 from the series called "Miserere" (Fig. 5): attempts to use his expressionist forms in order to make Christ's story present and contemporaneous to us. The last illustration I will cite is a "Crucifixion" by Rouault. I must repeat, sometimes I have the feeling that these are solutions, at least better ones than anything we have in the traditional "junk" of religious art today. But on the other hand, I ask myself, "Is the present day man really able to answer the question put before us by existentialism?"

EXISTENTIALISM AND IDEALIZED NATURALISM

Idealized naturalism still is the favorite form of art for many people. What does this favorite form mean from an existentialist point of view? It means the unwillingness to see and to face our real situation; therefore the relationship to modern art and its existentialist elements is a very serious affair. Let me tell you of an experience from my past after I had come out of the first World War, and the German Republic had been established. I was teaching at the University of Berlin, opposite the Museum of Modern Art just established by the newly formed republic. I myself used pictures in my lectures in order to show in other realms of life, especially philosophy, the relationship of form and substance, the possibility of breaking the surface form of reality in order to dig into its depths; and I must confess that I have not learned from any theological book as much as I learned from these pictures of the great modern artists who broke through into the realm out of which symbols are

born. And you cannot understand theology without understanding symbols. In this museum something happened every day. The petty bourgeoisie of Germany also
went to these exhibitions and I will never forget the
smiling and laughing, or hostile and malignant faces in
front of these pictures. What they expected in a museum
was idealized naturalism. These pictures, however, had
neither nature in the surface sense of the word in them,
nor idealizing beauty. Instead of this they had shocking
disruptions, distortions, elements of reality brought out
of the depths to the surface by the painter. These petty
people fought against this. This was, in the realm of art,
the fight between the coming Nazism, produced by the
same petty bourgeoisie, against the progressive intelligentsia which realized the dangerous situation in the
industrial society. The petty bourgeoisie did not want to
see that its situation had fundamentally changed, and
Fascism was the attempt to maintain the old situation by
means of suppression and terror. Now this shows that in
artistic problems, and especially in the problems of existentialism in art, all realms are somehow present. However, let me go back to the religious realm. What has
this situation to tell us about the religious realm and
about our human situation? It has to tell us, first of all,
that there are moments in individual life and in the life
of society when something cannot be hidden, cannot be
covered any more. If the surface is maintained, then this
can be done only at the price of honesty, of realism, of
looking into the depths of our situation, and this price
always includes fanaticism, repressing elements of truth,
and self-destruction. We must be able—and that was the
great work of these artists—to face our present reality as
what it is. These artists were accused by many of having only negative characteristics. Hitler piled up their

works in a museum of decadent art, a museum which contained some of the greatest treasures which later were brought to this country as great works of art. But as for Hitler, as a representative of the desperate petty bourgeoisie which wanted to keep itself in existence, he called this distorted, degenerated art. As long as we remove from our sight what we cannot help facing, we become dishonest; then that kind of art which he favored, that kind of beautifying realism, is what covers reality. These artists, therefore, who took away the cover from our situation, had a prophetic function in our time. I do not like all of them, either. But I know they created revealing works of art to look at which is the joy of participating in a level of reality which we otherwise can never reach.

And now finally about the relationship of the churches to all of this. The churches followed in most cases the petty bourgeoisie resistance against modern art and against existentialism generally. The churches believed they had all the answers. But in believing that they had all the answers they deprived the answers of their meaning. These answers were no longer understood because the questions were no longer understood, and this was the churches' fault. They did not do what the existentialist artist did. They did not ask the questions over again as they should have out of the experience of despair in industrial society. The churches did not ask the question, and therefore their answers, all the religious answers Christianity has in its creeds, became empty. Nobody knew what to do with them because the questions were not vivid any more as they were in the periods in which these answers were given. This, then, is my last statement about the whole thing. I believe that existentialist art has a tremendous religious function, in visual art as

well as in all other realms of art, namely, to rediscover
the basic questions to which the Christian symbols are
the answers in a way which is understandable to our
time. These symbols can then become again understandable to our time.

8. *On the Naming of the Gods in Hölderlin and Rilke*

We must now lift the cork even further from this care-fully bottled existentialism!—In this there lies a risk, for we know quite well that once the *geni* of this vaporous mystery of existence is released from the con-ventional structures in which we keep it so carefully bottled and so tightly sealed, we shall not recover it again until we learn something of the secret talisman which the powers of life obey.

Every existentialist proposition must bear, like the Dwarf on Zarathustra's shoulders, the burden of its own recoil. After every thrust of thinking it must tolerate the

whisper—"but upon *thyself* it will recoil." This is that
"wound of the negative," as Kierkegaard called it, which
it is the first task of the existentialist thinker to
keep open—for it is "sometimes the condition for a
cure."

Finally, we must accept Kierkegaard's familiar, and by
now conventional, recipe for all "existentialist" conclu-
sions: it must be *unscientific*—in order to avoid the trap
of the "system" and the temptation to volatilize concrete
responsibility into formal propositions which abstract
from our personal involvement in the world; and it must
be *postscriptive*—insofar as the foregoing statements
have been authentic transcripts of existence and insofar as the pretension to "objectivity" has been made
to give way before what Tillich calls our "ultimate
concern."

In short (and to reverse the order), we must attempt
a summation which is not formal, or which continues to
point at the existentialists, in favor of one which points
at that which the existentialists are pointing at. Such a
pointing is at once a pointing at ourselves and a pointing to the truth as a task which I am called to fulfill or
bear witness to. It is from just this kind of pointing, or
double-pointedness (*Doppeldeutigkeit*), that the "para-
doxicality" of existentialism, or the awkwardness of
speaking existentially, arises. For existentialism is an
attempt to describe the "truth" as it relates to the
"truth-er," or truth as a "truth-ing" (the only authentic
locus of the true thing): and this makes for a literary
awkwardness in that "philosophy" heretofore has taken
the easy way of formal speculation *about* the truth, as
though the truth were altogether something other than
ourselves and could be halved and quartered like a
melon or an orange. The truth with which we are really

concerned is the truth in which we are already and antecedently involved, and from which involvement we cannot exempt ourselves.

The philosopher in the first position is like the flea of Diogenes Laertius which, riding upon the axle of the swiftly moving chariot, contemplated the roadway behind, and, after meditating thereon for a suitable interval, exclaimed "My, what a dust I do raise!" For the philosopher to overlook the human predicament in such a way is a costly oversight. No matter how learned or dignified such a philosopher might be, it is a luxury we can no longer afford. The philosopher today is obliged to begin with the human situation and to extract "meaning" from a consideration of who we are, and where we are going (the question of man's destiny), and why, and how, and whether there is anything that we can, must, or ought to do about it. The existentialist seeks to reconstitute the questions in such a way as to avoid the classical oversight. He seeks to think the true at the point of his relation to it. The "meaning" of "reality" will be found, he is persuaded, through a careful scrutiny of the experienced content of his "encounters" with it. Thus the temptation of the traditional thinker has been to commit the inadvertence of thinking himself exempt from truth as a requirement because he has thought about it; the temptation of the existentialist is to become so enamoured with the perusal of the subjective features of his own encounters with truth that he commits the indiscretion of supposing that truth and his own subjective states are one and the same: he converts unwittingly, that is, the dialogue of his encounters with reality into a dialectical monologue with himself. Such are the extremes of awkwardness into which the student of these matters may fall.

Fortunately, however, there is another way. There are, in fact, three ways—the way of the saint, the way of the prophet, and the way of the poet. The saint *lives* his relation to the true, and so *exhibits* it. His life is the only adequate commentary upon it. The prophet *proclaims* it, as he feels the pressure of the Absolute upon himself and upon his time; he denounces, from the vantage point of the Eternal, the failures of the people. The poet *seeks* it, searching for the new meaning at the point where fresh suffering or fresh vision exposes the wound of the time; there he draws the "arrows of outrageous fortune" upon himself; he is wounded for our transgressions; he suffers it all, from the human side, in order to make himself open to the new meaning arising like the unacknowledged dawn upon what's next to be in the world. He becomes, after this fashion (sometimes unwittingly, sometimes witlessly), a "spiritual witness."

Kierkegaard understood these differences well. He would like to have been called an Apostle: but he realized that one cannot call oneself an Apostle without running the risk of becoming an Apostle of oneself, in which case one is no Apostle at all, but an egoistic charlatan of the spirit. He described himself, therefore, as a poet of the Eternal. Unamuno held that "philosophy lies closer to poetry than science." Most interesting of all, however, is the fact that Heidegger, in his later work (which marks a radical shift in his thinking), has turned to the work of the poet: particularly to the work of Hölderlin, and, still more recently (in the *Holzwege*), to Hölderlin and Rilke; and Gabriel Marcel, in his

Homo Viator, has devoted two of his happiest and most penetrating studies to the spiritual witness of Rilke.

This turning is of more than casual or marginal interest. It is far from accidental or fortuitous. We are here provided with an uncommonly clear approach to the inner relevance of existentialism as possibly the most significant spiritual phenomenon of these times.

"What is a poet?" asked Kierkegaard. And he answered:

> "A poet is an unhappy being whose heart is torn by secret sufferings, but whose lips are so strangely formed that when the sighs and cries escape them, they sound like beautiful music. His fate is like that of the unfortunate victims whom the tyrant Phalaris imprisoned in a brazen bull, and slowly tortured over a steady fire; their cries could not reach the tyrant's ears so as to strike terror into his heart: when they reached his ears they sounded like sweet music. And men crowd about the poet and say to him: 'You must sing for us again soon.' Which is as much to say, 'May fresh sufferings torture your soul, but may your lips be formed as before; for the cries would only frighten us, but the music is delicious.' " [1]

Such, indeed was the poet Hölderlin—who suffered pathetically but whose cries were transformed into a delicious music. Less evidently, but in a quite different way, the same might be said of Rilke.

The specific pattern of these sufferings need not concern us closely. We are not speaking primarily of Hölderlin and Rilke, but of an aspect of their work which has become prominent in the reflections of Heidegger and Marcel, and about the possible significance of this for an understanding and evaluation of existentialism as a whole.

Biographically, it may be useful to note, in the words of a New York reviewer, that "the great doomed poets of Romanticism, *les poets maudits,* Hölderlin, Daudelaire, Poe, Rimbaud, were (all) tormented by their mothers. . . . All of them were hag-ridden by female super-egos of exceptional ferocity!" After this bit of exceptional rhetoric, set forth with almost autochthonic spleen, as though the reviewer had stumbled suddenly upon the true origin of Original Sin, his line relaxes—and he continues, somewhat pathetically, but with calm of mind, all passion of his protest spent:

> "Only Hölderlin went completely mad. By the time he was 32 his literary career was over. He spent his remaining forty-one years in confinement, with a workman for a keeper, idling in his garden, pounding his piano, babbling to the great and the curious who visited him, and whom he invariably addressed as 'Your Majesty' or 'Your Highness.' "

> "For all the devotion he inspired in simpler people, his peers, actually his inferiors, treated him as a half pariah. Goethe and Schiller looked on him as a comic and embarrassing oddity. Today his poetry has more to say to the contemporary mind than all their vast and sometimes banal accomplishments." [2]

This is really all that we need to know (for our present purpose) about Hölderlin. We might add simply that he was born in 1770—the year in which Immanuel Kant was appointed Ordinary Professor of Logic and Metaphysics in the University of Königsberg; that he matriculated as a theological student at Tübingen, where he prepared and delivered sermons regularly, became closely acquainted with Hegel and Schelling, and wrote letters to his mother trying to persuade her he was meant to be a poet and not a clergyman.

Rilke clearly belongs—and quite profoundly—in this succession. Charles du Bois, building upon Keats, speaks of "the valley where souls are fashioned, wherein intelligence is put to the test and made into a soul." [3] Marcel quotes this statement as one that Rilke would have subscribed to heartily, and comments on the everywhere

evident fact that Rilke's poems "ring with the marvel-
lously fraternal understanding which souls cruelly
wounded in life's journey find in them." This is at once
the wound of Baudelaire ("His soul was born with a
scar." Sainte-Beuve); and of Jacob; and of Adam—that
is to say, the rest of us.

Rilke is also nearer to us in point of time (1875–
1926); but there is a point where the deep concerns of
Heidegger and Hölderlin, Marcel and Rilke intersect.
This is a point in height and depth. It is a point where
the non-Christian, Heidegger, ventures into the open
unknown with the Christian poet, Hölderlin; and a
point where the Christian philosopher, Marcel, explores
the spiritual witness of the non-Christian poet, Rilke. It
is a point where the term "Christian" is deprived of
its provincial and conventional structures and where its
living essence must be sought. Of all the so-called "paradoxes" of existentialist belief, this one is the most au-
dacious. For it requires that the believer (not the unbe-
liever) must effect that "willing suspension" not of
disbelief but of *belief* in order to let go of a security
system that no longer sustains: otherwise he is an idola-
tor and no true believer. The ultimate test of the authenticity of one's beliefs consists in this: that the believer
have *faith* enough to suspend the forms of his beliefs on
behalf of the integrity of his spiritual witness.

This is the challenge of existentialism. In its most
dramatic form it presupposes what Nietzsche called "the
death of God." Zarathustra's comment on the old man of
the forest might well be taken as Nietzsche's epigraph
for the nineteenth-century consciousness: "*Dieser alte
Heilige hat in seinem Walde noch nichts davon gehört,
dass Gott tot ist!*"—Could it be possible! This old saint
in his forest hath not yet heard that God is dead! Heine

had observed this before him, and Jean Paul Richter: just as Sartre and Heidegger note it after him. The God that had died for Nietzsche was the God of Christendom, together with the moral attitude and the mental outlook which went with it. It was not, therefore, that he found no God, but that he could not feel "that what has been revered as God is 'godlike.' " Nietzsche's protest is, therefore, on its negative side, similar to Kierkegaard's attack on Christendom. Kierkegaard knew that he had to break up Christianity's identification with Christendom in order "to reintroduce Christianity into Christendom." *Both* protests are anti-intellectualistic, in the philosophical sense, and point to the collapse and slow demise of a world-view and a culture consciousness which, for centuries, had sought to bind Christianity to substantialistic metaphysics. In this sense, *both* protests, and existentialism generally, must be viewed as (at bottom) a continuation of the Protestant protest.

Heidegger is at once more judicious, and more philosophical, when, by abandoning the declarative mood of the prophet (Nietzsche and Kierkegaard), he chooses the seeking mood of the poet. It is the poet who senses the deep and unacknowledged agony in the heart of man. It is the poet who probes the loneliness, the lostness, the inner mysteries in search of a true and authentic word of the Real. It is the poet (as in Dante, Eliot, Auden) who recognizes, and concedes, that we are lost in the woods:

> "Alone, alone, about a dreadful wood
> Of conscious evil runs a lost mankind,
> Dreading to find its Father lest it find
> The Goodness it has dreaded is not good:
> Alone, alone, about a dreadful wood. . . ."
> (Auden: *For the Time Being*)

Thus Heidegger (in *Holzwege*) recognizes that we are today in the deep woods where the familiar trails to reality are swallowed up in thickets of confusion: the spoors are thickly overlaid, and what we seek is some fresh track, some footprint of the gods, which may lead us out of the darkness and out of our time of spiritual dearth.

THE GODLY IMMANENCE

Wherefore the poet, then, in a time of dearth? asks Heidegger in the words of Hölderlin. Heidegger's answer, by way of Hölderlin and Rilke, would seem to be two-fold: it is (1) that in the time of dearth when God has died, and sufferings are not understood, and love is not learned,

> "Only song over the land
> hallows and celebrates."
> (Rilke: *Sonnets to Orpheus*, I, 19)

And (2), this very search for the holy on the part of the poet leads him out beyond the precincts of "God's failure" (the failure of the conventions of form and speech and pattern in which we have found Him) into the "open"—where the new name of God may be learned. This naming of the God need not be a direct naming—a naming in form; it will more than likely be a naming in depth, where the poet's ability to experience (both in the agony of his search and in the anguish of his creative task) the pressures of the open encounter with the Real, converts both his life and his work into an allegory (or a cipher) of something larger. Marcel's view of the "spiritual witness" is like this: an authentic spiritual witness is "one who testifies, and (whose) testimony is not a mere echo, (but) is a participation and a confirmation; to bear witness is to contribute to the growth or coming of that for which one testifies." [4]

Two themes, therefore, recurrent in Hölderlin, are of the greatest possible significance—the first not obviously so, the theme of homecoming; and the second, unavoidably so, the theme of the naming of the gods. These two themes, which appear to stand in separateness over against each other, are in fact, as will be seen, not separated at all, but are one in essence, and are, at bottom, compounded in the same spiritual movement.

1. *Homecoming.* This is already evident in Hölderlin's elegy entitled *Homecoming,* in which the wanderer (symbol of our spiritual alienation) is seen returning to the land of his birth. But home is not easy to gain. The familiar remains the remote. The gap of our wanderings lies between what *was* and what *is.* Therefore the homecoming is still a journey. It is a journey which begins like that of Abraham, but ends like that of the Prodigal. The true home-coming "really consists (writes Heidegger) solely in the people of the country becoming at home in the still-withheld essence of home"—or, more simply, "learning at home to be at home."

The paradox of such journeying is already apparent on the surface. Clearly there is a sense in which we have always been at the point at which we are arriving, and yet we have never been there except in the sense that it is at this point that we are perpetually arriving. The being is in the arriving. It is a journey to where we are. But where we *are* is where we are becoming what we are capable of becoming—where what we are (under God) is being lived into its true calling, the godly gift not being denied, but being produced with daring and courage and fidelity of trust into the forms of that which is

authentically latent within us, or into the image of the
god that is already coming to meet us.

> "That which thou seekest is near, and already
> coming to meet thee."

This is the startling affirmation arising out of the poet's
journey into the paradox; but that which prevents the
fullness of return is the estranging fact that "holy names
are lacking." In the time of dearth we remain strangers
to one another and to all that is familiar because the
holy names are lacking, because of the absence of God.

The true homecoming must be therefore, most deeply,
a return into the *proximity* of the *source* (the god is
near, he is coming) : we may not make idols, which prevents the return; and we may not call upon an accustomed god, a dogma, or a form, which always prepares
and then perpetuates the exile. The poet's vocation is to
divest himself of the protective systems which have kept
the god out: and "without fear of the appearance of godlessness he must remain near the failure of the god (to
come), and wait long enough in the prepared proximity
of the failure, until out of the proximity of the failing
god the initial word is granted, which names the High
One" (Heidegger).[5]

Two things may be noted here. As Gustav Thibon
phrases it, "the absence of God moves about here with
the intimacy of a presence." The unrecognized Biblical
perspectives which are everywhere pervasive of both
poem and analysis are startling. The familiar theme of
"return" in Jeremiah, for instance, is only superficially
a counsel of geographical return from exile: it is essentially an imperative of return to the source of all well-
being for Jeremiah, a return to the open fidelity to
Yahweh which characterized the life of the people in

the wilderness, when the people were to Yahweh as a
bride is to her husband (Jer. 2:2). The risks of the appearance of godlessness are like those of Job, who had
discovered that the conventional forms (the names of
God) were empty and his time a time of dearth. "The
metaphysics of restlessness thus appears as the normal
movement of the soul *naturaliter* Christian" (Thibon).[6]

2. *Naming the Gods.* The second thing is that the
inner aspiration here is "to name the High One." This
Heidegger is trying to do, by moving out, like Job, into
the proximity to the source. This Hölderlin also aimed
at, although the conditions were hard. In his poem, *The
Poet's Vocation,* he writes:

> "But fearless man remains, as he must,
>   Alone before God, simplicity protects him,
>   And no weapon needs he, and no
>   Cunning, till the time when God's failure helps."

To be fearless, and alone before God, is difficult. Simplicity also is difficult. But at the point where one out-
grows the protective conventions, and at the point where
"the Time" collapses into the vacuum at the heart of
its inherited pretensions, there "God's failure" helps.
Some there are who must undertake the venture into
the proximity of our primary meanings. It is "cares like
these" that the singer "must bear in his soul and often."
Such a poet "compels a decision."

But at what points is decision required? Surely at the
point of his doctrine of the source and the poet's proximity to it:

> "that which thou seekest is near, and
>   already (it is) running to meet thee, . . ."

—as though the god were about to appear, the new god,
the new center around which a new epoch might be
built; or as though the source were somehow within the

being within which we are existents, and that the being
will come into existence as we succeed in converting our
present being (which has become a nothingness) into a
positive nothingness out of which the new may come
into existence.

This sounds like Hegel of course, though it is qualitatively different. Nevertheless, if Hegel's logic could be
existentialized there would emerge a sharp parallel. I
should discover (1) that my tendency is to consolidate
and fasten upon such existence as I have wrested from
circumstance, and to abide in it (as my thesis for life);
but life moves on, and out from under my "system,"
and I am left with the dialectical emptiness, the carcass,
of my system. Thus it becomes necessary (2) for me to
discover existentially that precisely this hardening is
not permitted: that I, if I am to exist (or, in Kierkegaard's sense, to "become"), must negate (antithesis)
the fixation of my own being, in order that the authentic existent may appear. For I discover that if I do not
do this, *it is done to me:* nothingness infiltrates my
existence; for my existence has become an idol, a form,
which, if I am not imposing it on others, I am nevertheless coercing it upon myself. I thus become emptied,
and the desperate encounter with nothingness—nega-
tively understood—begins. But this is the beginning (if
I accept it positively as a task and a calling) of the third
term (the synthesis). But such a third term is no synthesis (on the level of Hegel's principle of mediation);
it is the actualization of what has merely been latent
before; or, if the dimension is ultimate, it is the New
Being of which the Scriptures speak.

But this brings us to the second point at which Hölderlin (and Heidegger by way of Hölderlin) compels a
decision: the mystery of the godly immanence that is
here supposed.

This is to be distinguished from "mysticism," on the one hand, and from "pantheism" on the other. The mystery of the godly immanence compels a decision in a qualitatively different way. This way we discover by noting the hidden and smothered persistence of Hölderlin's problem throughout the witness of western thought. Hölderlin's paradox—

> "That which thou seekest is near, and
> already coming to meet thee—"

is similar, in its depth implication, to Pascal's *Mystery of Jesus—*

> "Console thyself (says Jesus), thou wouldst not be
> seeking me hadst thou not already found me."[8]

It has also affinities with Augustine's confession (X. xx. 29):

> "How, then do I seek thee, Lord? For when I seek Thee, my God, I seek a happy life. . . . (But) how do I seek it? Is it by remembrance, as though I had forgotten it, knowing too that I had forgotten it? . . . Truly we have it, but how I know not. . . . For did we not know it, we should not love it."

Clearly this is a parallelism of a profound and far-reaching kind. It could open up in several directions.

It could move back to Plato's "pugnacious proposition" of the *Meno:*

> "One cannot seek for what he knows, and it seems equally impossible for him to seek for what he does not know. For what a man knows he cannot seek, since he knows it; and what he does not know he cannot seek, since he does not even know for what to seek." (80)

Plato concludes from this that knowledge is something we already possess: we have it already in mind as thinking power. We have only *forgotten* the true knowledge and become victimized by the secondary world of opinions: we must therefore be led to *recollect* the source

from which we have come. This opens the path to intellectualism, or the path to mysticism.

It could also move into simple Biblical existentialism,
where that which we seek is near, and already coming
to meet us:

> "Ask and the gift will be yours,
>   seek and you will find,
>   knock and the door will open to you." . . .(Mt. 7:7,
>   Moffatt)

Since, however, the simple Biblical assurance that God
has provided us with all that we have need of, offends us
in its simplicity and in its simple requirement of faithful seeking and trust, we complicate the issue—that is to
say, ourselves—and so produce the vast complicities of
"evil."

The mystery of godly immanence opens therefore also
into a deeper view of the self. Augustine's view of God
as the indwelling power of the true self again coincides
with this:

> "Behold, Thou wert within, and I without, and there did I seek
> thee: I, unlovely, rushed heedlessly among the things of beauty
> Thou madest. Thou wert with me, but I was not with Thee." [9]

It is in this sense that Jeremiah's witness must be understood:

> "I know, O LORD, that the way of man is not in himself,
>   that it is not in man who walks to direct his steps." . . .
>   (Jer. 10:23, RSV)

The man who does not learn how to rest upon the godly
immanence will "be brought to nothing." Which is the
inner core, also, of Kierkegaard's protracted claim that
the self becomes a self only through founding itself

transparently upon the power that created it. If we *could* turn from the far countries of Nothingness, where emptiness and meaninglessness and vanities gather, and return into our true selves and found ourselves transparently upon the power that perpetually creates us and sustains us, would this not come near to the *homecoming* of which Hölderlin speaks, and would it not be a return to the proximity of the *source* which seems so compelling to Heidegger?

There is, in this connection, an important passage in Marcel:

> "I have spoken (he writes) of the incarnation in a sense purely philosophical; this incarnation, mine, yours, is to the other Incarnation, to the dogma of the Incarnation, that which the philosophical mysteries are to the revealed mysteries." [10]

Gustav Thibon's comment and question ties this in sharply with the foregoing:

> "But these two orders of mysteries, are they not concretely united at the foundation of the soul created for God, and which, without knowing it, searches for God?" [10]

To confirm this view (which clearly is based upon Augustine's formula for all Christian existentialism: to wit, "Thou has made us for Thyself, and our hearts are restless until they find their rest in Thee"), he quotes Marcel again:

> "A concrete philosophy is not able NOT to be magnetized, perhaps without its own knowledge, by the Christian gifts. . . . For a Christian, there exists an essential conformity between Christianity and human nature. Thus, the more profoundly we penetrate into human nature, the more we place ourselves within the axis of the great Christian truths. But someone will object: you say this as a Christian, not as a philosopher. I am able to recall only what I said

at the beginning: the philosopher who constrains himself to think only as a philosopher places himself outside of experience, in an infra-human realm: but philosophy is a raising up of experience, it is not its castration." [11]

Thus the first theme which challenges Heidegger—that of *homecoming*—leads by way of the metaphor of journey and return into the questions of return to the source and the nature of the godly immanence experienced in this return. The classical appraisals lead away unfaithfully from this experience into the abstract forms of the infra-human realms; the existentialist journeys more faithfully into the self, placing himself, whether wittingly or no, within the axis of the great Christian truths.

3. *The Poet's Mission.* The most startling overlap with Rilke appears, however, in the second theme which challenges Heidegger (and which also compels a decision): namely, that of the naming of the gods. Hölderlin's *Patmos* hymn, which has been pronounced "the most profoundly Christian of Hölderlin's hymns" and his "consummate achievement," begins impressively:

> "Near and
> Hard to grasp is the god.
> But where danger is,
> The deliverer too grows strong."

The first two lines are said to contain the essence of Hölderlin's poetic doctrine. They are strikingly similar to the paradox of homecoming, explored above. Here, however, the interest turns, not upon homecoming, but upon the poet's vocation—his call to venture (when the time of "God's failure" helps) out into the open, there to await in patience the new apprehension of the nature of God.

This is a dangerous, sometimes a desperate, venture. Its nature Hölderlin describes in the lines which follow:

> "In the darkness dwell
> The eagles and fearless
> The sons of the Alps go out over the abyss
> On lightly built bridges.
> Therefore, since massed around are
> The peaks of time
> And the dear ones dwell near to one another,
> Tired on mountains farthest apart,
> Grant innocent water,
> O give us wings, to go over
> Loyal-mindedly and return."

Everyone knows something of the pathos of this separateness. Heaped as we are on the summits of Time, and dwelling like the Alpine peaks in proximate community, we live none the less on deeply separated mountains. We have neither the wings of understanding wherewith to cross over to one another, nor do we possess that spontaneity of open motives whereby we might go over loyal-mindedly and return. The depth of the abyss between us deepens with the death of God, or in any epoch where "holy names are lacking." In the time of dearth it is the poet who must go—whether like Jacob, or Job, or Elijah —to grasp the god.

That it is the poet who must go arises from Hölderlin's persuasion that language and the art of words, which appears to be the "most innocent of all occupations"—like a game almost—is in reality the "most dangerous of possessions." It is by way of language that "we become a conversation." By language community is established. It is in the word that we meet, as Buber might put it: the true community is between us. But it is by language that we produce a world, and only where

world is, is there a history, and only where history is, is
there a destiny. It is in relation to this last that there
arises the most solemn possibility of all, namely, that it
is by way of language that we are enabled to name the
gods. "Poetry is the act of establishing by the word and
in the word," remarks Heidegger.

The dangers here are manifold. There is the danger
that the poet who assumes this mission may not have
the psychical strength to encounter the god. "Human
kind cannot bear very much reality," as Eliot says. There
is the danger too that one may encounter a demon and
be overborne by him, as was very possibly the case with
Hölderlin. There is also the danger of naming the gods
wrongly, of misconstruing their meaning, and so of intro-
ducing confusion into world and history and destiny.
Language may thus menace the human condition. It may
threaten existence. Language is thus the most dangerous
of human possessions. This danger is further augmented
by the fact that "the first-fruits (of speech with the
gods) are never for mortals" but must be made more
ordinary, more familiar and everyday, for the people.
But the counterfeit apes the true; it is not always easy to
distinguish the essential word from the non-essential.
The counterfeit may parade as the authentic: it may
even be celebrated as such, and fasten its forms and re-
quirements upon the people in the open tyrannies of
hallowed norms. These become the existent, and people
cling to them because they are the existent and because
they are hallowed. Thus the existent closes out the gods
and becomes a constricting threat to existence. "Being
must be opened out, so that the existent may appear,"
interprets Heidegger. But this is dangerous. Nevertheless, in a time of dearth, it is just this manifold risk that
the poet must run.

Hölderlin himself was not equal to it. Too late he learned that

> ". . . where danger is
> The deliverer too grows strong."

Already he was enmeshed in the regressive estrangement from reality. He betrays, says Jung, "the secret longing for the maternal depths." His quest for the new name of the god volatilizes into a vagueness—the vagueness of his own myth projection. He sank into his own depths longing retrospectively for Icarus' wings: or better, he walked bravely into the darkness of Peniel, but, at precisely the point where he should have grappled with God's angel, he wandered away dreaming that that which he sought was already coming to meet him, but at a point of his own choosing rather than of God's. Thus was there no meeting—only the shadows of meeting. He went down, like Orpheus, into the Hades of the Holy Night, singing: Persephone was enchanted with his singing; but the poet was enchanted by her enchantment, and so remained there—singing.

> "For a weak vessel cannot always receive them [the gods],
> Only at times can mankind bear the full weight of the gods.
> Life [for most] is a dream of them. . . ."
> *(Bread and Wine,* VII)

That Hölderlin understood the risks of such a venture, and that he came very near to the precincts of Grace at times, is not to be denied. He sensed that

> ". . . the serving maids of Heaven
> Are miraculous,
> Like all that's a heavenly birth.
> He who would grasp it by stealth

> Holds a dream in his hand, and him who attempts
> To grow like it by force, it punishes.
> Yet often it takes by surprise
> Him who has hardly begun to give it a thought."
>
> *(The Journey)*

Greater souls than Hölderlin have found the journey difficult. Jeremiah, a poet, felt and responded to such a call—though it led him into fear and trembling bordering on psychological "breakdown": but he moved out from under the compounded fixations of his time, and into the open, where he came under the ineluctable hold of the Creator in such a way as to rename the god in terms of the New Covenant, a covenant written in the heart. Job, also, outgrew the conventional name of God. He suffered aloneness, and alone suffered—risking the storms of God, who, as Elihu shrewdly perceived, was already speaking to him through his dreams and through his pain. These knew, as Hölderlin came to know, that

> ". . . it behoves us, under the storms of God
> Ye poets! with uncovered head to stand.
> With our own hand to grasp the very lightning-flash
> Paternal, and to pass, wrapped in song,
> The divine gift to the people."
>
> *(Wie wenn am Feierstage)*

The poet himself stands, says Heidegger, "between the gods and the people. He is the one who has been cast out —out into that *Between,* between gods and men. But only and for the first time in this Between is it decided, who man is and where he is settling his existence." [12]

We must bear in mind now, that the presupposition of this interpretation is that ours is a time of dearth, that our gods have failed and therefore the God is withdrawn. This is at the same time (for Heidegger) a sign and promise of hope:

"It is the time of the gods that have fled *and* of the god that is coming. It is the time of *need,* because it lies under a double lack and a double Not: the No-more of the gods that have fled and the Not-yet of the god that is coming." [13]

Others have intuited this. Matthew Arnold's

> "Wandering between two worlds, one dead
> The other powerless to be born"

evokes the same dilemma. Flaubert remarked of a similar parenthesis in ancient times: "The gods being no more and Christ being not yet, there was between Cicero and Marcus Aurelius a unique moment in which man stood alone." This is again the moment of the time of dearth, and though dangerous and difficult in itself, it is nevertheless big with the promise of the conditions for a fresh awareness of the nature of the true. Hölderlin was not, perhaps the poet of this time; but he was, at least, holds Heidegger, the "forerunner" of the poet of the time of dearth.

THROUGH DESCENT TO ASCENT

Heidegger's appeal to Rilke is a sound one. When Heidegger read the *Elegies* he felt that Rilke had sung in his poetry what he had written in his *Sein und Zeit.* In Rilke "the word of the singer retains still the track of the Holy." Therefore we look again for some fresh track out of the woods.

Heidegger's view of the poet's vocation is similar to that of Carl Jung: "Poets are the first in their time to divine the darkly moving, mysterious currents, and to express them according to the limits of their capacity in more or less speaking symbols. They make known, like

true prophets, the deep motions of the collective un-
conscious, 'the will of God' . . . which, in the course of
time, must inevitably come to the surface as a general
phenomenon." The publication of Rilke's *Sonnets to
Orpheus* and the *Elegies* in 1923, the appearance of
Franz Kafka's three novels soon after his death in 1924,
the printing of Heidegger's *Sein und Zeit* (1927) and
the great three-volume *Philosophie* of Jaspers in 1932,
to say nothing of the rise of dialectical theology in Germany and Switzerland, marks an elaborate transition in
continental thinking. Rilke's reading of Kierkegaard
belongs to this impressive upsurge of existential thinking.[14] Rilke as the poet of this "general phenomenon,"
also "compels a decision."

But again we must ask at what points does he compel
a decision: and again we must answer, at the point of
his doctrine of the godly immanence, and at the point
of his naming of the gods. At the point where Hölderlin
failed, Rilke picks up the fluttering torch and carries it
praisingly into the time's abyss. So courageously did he
carry it that he becomes for Eric Knight, the finest example of "the dedicated life in poetry"—one who "is
fundamentally a religious poet" whose "basic sacrifice
was made on the altar of his art, even if the fragrance
of it rose to Heaven."[15] For Gabriel Marcel he is "a
witness to the spiritual—one who testifies and (whose)
testimony is not a mere echo, (but) is a participation
and a confirmation."[16] For Heidegger he is the poet of
the time of dearth, our time, of which Hölderlin was but
the forerunner.

But here we must begin to distinguish; for surely
Rilke does not mean the same to Marcel and to Heidegger? and surely Hölderlin's journey into the "Between"
is somehow other than Rilke's journey? The themes are

proximate, it is true, and both Marcel and Heidegger rehearse the familiar Rilkean "groundterms"—Nature, Farewell, Relatedness, the World of Inwardness (*Weltinnenraum*), the Open, the Risk, the Angel, the all-pervading paradox of Life and Death and Love and Pain. Hurled as we are into existence (Heidegger) the risk is unavoidable. Rilke's venture into the depth dimension of our inwardness confirms this. Where risk is there danger is. But where existence is there risk is. It is by way of the faithful acceptance of existence as a risk that one begins to discover a foothold in reality—"within the sphere of subjectivity as that of the inner and invisible Presence." [17] In this movement we pass through the ground of existence to the very ground of Being.[18]

Now there can be no doubt but that it is the inner and invisible Presence for which Heidegger and Hölderlin are searching: but it is this precisely which is absent from Heidegger and leaves his philosophy an "existence unto death," and it is this which is present to Rilke lending warmth to his poetry and giving it the sustaining and consoling properties that it has.

These are subtle differences (but far-reaching ones) which may be traced in the hovering of metaphors.

Both for Heidegger and for Rilke man must become "the shepherd of Being." Those who are chosen "to attain the purest"

> ". . . must stand like the shepherd, outlasting,
> from afar it may seem that he mourns,
> coming nearer one feels how he watches."
> (Rilke, *Lines of the 10th August*)

One feels how Heidegger watches, sounding with Hölderlin the mystery of distance and emptiness (Nothingness). But Rilke's watching is at once more realistic

than Hölderlin's and more Biblical than Heidegger's.
He had learned from Rodin how to work, so his watching is not passive: he had learned from the toils of his
vocation how to wait with patience—how to "wait upon
the Lord," upon a *kairos* of grace, in which, as watcher,
he suffers his experience to ripen in secret until that
peculiar fullness of time when suddenly its meaning
comes clear.

> "He who for the first time has Thee in his keeping
> is disturbed by his neighbour, or his watch;
> he walks bent over Thy footprints,
> as if laden and burdened with years.
> Only later does he draw near to nature,
> becomes aware of the winds and the far distances,
> hears Thy whisper in the meadow,
> worships Thee in song from the stars,
> and can never again unlearn Thee,
> for everything is but Thy mantle." [19]

One feels that Heidegger, as shepherd, watches and waits
in an emptiness, formulating its problem: Rilke watches
and waits as one surrounded by a Presence, beholding its
mystery, convinced that God is

> ". . . new and near and good
> and marvellous as a journey."

Hölderlin, in his turn, does not wait as a shepherd.
When he waits, he waits as one who must go on a journey—a journey into abysses, a journey fraught with
danger, a danger akin to that which Heraclitus knew:
"the journey to the self is a journey without return." He
discovered too late that

> ". . . where danger is
> The deliverer too grows strong. . . .";

but he does not reveal this as a knowledge (in Rilke's sense) or as a possession. Rilke speaks more surely:

"We have no reason to mistrust our world (he wrote to the young theological student who sought his advice), for it is not against us. Has it terrors, they are *our* terrors; has it abysses, those abysses belong to us; are dangers at hand, we must try to love them. And if we only . . . hold to what is difficult, then that which now still seems to us most hostile, will become what we most trust and find most faithful. . . . Those ancient myths . . . about dragons that at the last moment turn into princesses; perhaps all the dragons of our lives are princesses who are only waiting to see us once beautiful and brave. Perhaps everything terrible is in its deepest being something helpless that wants help from us." [20]

And the note of patience is enjoined:

"Be patient towards all that is unsolved in your heart and try to love THE QUESTIONS THEMSELVES like locked rooms. . . . Do not now seek the answers, that cannot be given you because you would not be able to live them. And the point is, to live everything. *Live* the questions now. Perhaps you will then gradually, without noticing it, live along some distant day into the answer." [21]

The relation between patience and Presence is also expressed:

"I must wait for the ringing in the silence. . . . Sometimes it is thus and I am master of my depths, which open out radiant and beautiful and shimmering in the darkness; but it is not I that have said the magic Word; God says it when it is time, and it is meet for me only to be patient and to wait and to suffer my depths trustingly." [22]

It begins to appear that the metaphor of shepherding is not adequate. Heidegger watches not so much like a shepherd as like one of the ancient Magi, studying the heavens for some fresh confluence of metaphysical symbols which might set him journeying into adoration and truth. He ignores, meanwhile, "the Galilean turbulence" (Yeats) which

> "Made all Platonic tolerance vain
> And vain all Doric discipline"

and remains like Eliot's Magi, "no longer at ease here, in the old dispensation," probing a Being under the metaphysical signature of "another death." [23]

Hölderlin meanwhile sought to go over the abysses on Icarus wings. Rilke, more realistically, accepts the Orpheus descent into Hades as the necessary presupposition of all authentic creative return. Almost everything in Rilke is contained within the rubric of this Orpheus descent.

There are three moments in the journey.

There is, first, the acceptance of descent. It begins where we are, in our present world.

> "*Here* is the time of the *sayable, here* is its home."
>
> (*Elegies*, IX)

The movement begins, therefore, not as a flight from one's self, or from the predicament, but moves precisely into it. This movement is a risk, but it is necessary:

> "That which would stay what it is renounces existence. . . ."
>
> (*Sonnets* II, 12)

All the existentialists know this: but Rilke knew that this movement, if chosen faithfully, was a movement into a Presence—though it might entail the descent into Hell, or the encounters with the negative, or with Tillich's non-being and its threats of fate, death, emptiness, meaningless, guilt and condemnation; or with Jasper's limit-situations of struggle, suffering, guilt and

death; or with "the mountains of Primal Pain." Behind
and beyond all these threats to my being "something is
hiding."

While this Presence is outside us and other than us, it
is nevertheless within us—is, indeed, the godly immanence—and we must understand the self accordingly.

"It seems to me more and more (wrote Rilke in a passage quoted
both by Heidegger and Marcel) as though our ordinary consciousness dwelt on the summit of a pyramid whose base broadens out in
us and beneath us so much that the more deeply we see ourselves
able to penetrate into it the more boundlessly do we seem impli-
cated in these factors of our earthly, and in the widest sense, *worldly*
being which are independent of space and time. Since my earliest
youth I have entertained the idea (and have also, when I was adequate to it, lived accordingly), that if a cross-section were made
lower down through this pyramid of consciousness, Being, in its
simplest form, would become 'eventual' in us, the inviolable
presence and simultaneity of all that we, on the upper 'normal'
apex of consciousness, are only permitted to experience as flux
(Ablauf)." [24]

Not only does this interesting statement assert a dimension of transcendence and a metaphysic of Being, it confirms also the paradox of the self understood as spirit—
Kierkegaard's view that the self can become a self only
by grounding itself upon the power that created it.

Indeed, the Kierkegaardian dimension is retained
here. The imperative that we must choose ourselves absolutely appears, in Rilke's terms—

"Choose to be changed. With the flame be enraptured, where
from within you a thing changefully—splendid escapes."
                                                    (*Sonnets* II, 12)

There is, however, an added dimension. Whereas
Kierkegaard's "leap" of faith remains barren, resolving
itself as a leap into dogmatic emptiness, Rilke's move-

ment bases itself (1) upon a primary receptivity, and
(2) upon a metamorphosis and fruition of return. The
"encounters" of life want, he says, "rather to be suffered
than acknowledged . . . ; rather consented to and loved
than questioned and made use of. . . . It belongs to the
original tendencies of my nature to accept the Mysterious *as such*, not as something to be exposed, but as the
Mystery that is mysterious to its very depths and is so
everywhere. . . ." [25] It is this "receptivity," this attitude
of acceptance, which Marcel regards as "really creation
itself under another name. The most genuinely receptive
being is at the same time the most essentially creative. . . ." [26] And he adds that this is a truth which
Nietzsche and Kierkegaard have generally "either never
known or in the end forgotten."

This metamorphosis is, in fact, the second movement
in Rilke's descent. What it supposes is "a night of universal blossoming" at the innermost limit of descent
where one will rediscover the openness of childhood,
established by grace. This is what Rilke aspired to—

"and make me thy minstrel, the baptist of this new messiah-
ship . . ."

Thence the ascent (the third movement) begins.

Everything in Rilke now focuses. His vocation as poet
lies beyond the metamorphosis, or is, at any rate,
always *effecting it*, and so moving upward on the steep
ascents of his return. He would be as Orpheus, mounting
with praise, singing life and love in the movement of
victory over nothingness and death. His eyes must be
forward, gazing into the open, trusting that all goodness
and charity follows behind him as he sings. To doubt,
to look back (the glance backward into death) is to
lose all.

It is in this context that we are "bees of the invisible" and must gather the honey of the tangible and work it up into the golden significances of the infinite related-ness of things. Both Heidegger and Marcel refer to this approvingly. Heidegger penetrates its meaning farther than many critics, who see in it little more than a poetized and incipient Platonism. Heidegger attaches it to the Re-collecting, or the re-cognition (*Die Er-inner-ung*) of the tangible within the heart space of con-sciousness where it is converted into the symbols of openness: by which movement we become free. But Rilke goes farther. Everything, for him, awaits this rescue; apart from it (since man is the creature of trans-cendence) all things "live on departure."

> "Earth, isn't this what you want: an invisible
> re-arising in us? . . . .
> . . . .
> What is your urgent command, if not transformation?"
> (*Elegies*, IX)

And again: "where I create I am true, and I want to find the strength to build my life wholly upon this truth, upon this infinite simplicity and joy that is some-times given me. . . ."

It becomes clear from this that the real opposition in Rilke is that between Life (or Love) and Death, and our task is to effect perpetually the transmutation (or, as Berdyaev would say, the transfiguration) of the mo-mentums of death into the resurrections of Life. How near he comes to Christianity has been traced by Alfred Focke,[27] who reminds us of the Johannine teaching: "God is love; and he that dwelleth in love dwelleth in God, and God in him. . . . He that loveth not . . . abideth in death (1 John 4:16; 3:14)." To this profoundest practical truth of the Gospels Rilke is a spiritual witness. He stands very near to Christianity. *Er hat aber nicht mehr den letzten Schritt getan*—but the last step he has not taken! We may well ask, why?

The answer will be found the moment we turn to the question of the naming of the gods in Rilke.

Because of his early conditioning (into which we may not venture here) Christianity repelled him. People who protested a great knowledge of God failed to fit themselves to Him productively. The Church had "pirated" and "pawned" everything God-given in the Creation into a nebulous "Beyond," whereas, for Rilke, everything must be "deeply and passionately (lived into) *here.*" The appeal to "faith," as used by Christians, he had found to be an unfaithful and compulsive appeal. "This forcing of the heart to regard this and that as true, which is ordinarily called Faith, has no sense. First you must find God somewhere, experience him as infinitely, prodigiously, stupendously present"—then, "there is no more stopping, no matter in what place you have begun." [28] Love must supersede "faith" or faith is not real. The terms "sin" and "redemption," as "preconditions of God" were somehow sacrilegious: they become "more and more repugnant to a heart that has understood the earth." So also the appeal to "Christian experience" was unconvincing, for "the primordial God-head outweighs it infinitely." Christ also, as he is worshipped, stands between us and God preventing our movement into the open, and bending us in upon the closed world of descent into death.

These are conventional protests. They do not go to the root of the matter. It would be easy, on the basis of these protests, to dismiss Rilke's view of Christianity as a diminished and truncated one, and so dispense with the prophetic element in his spiritual vision. They are, however, of considerable importance when seen from within that vision itself. They are the outward evidence of an inner momentum towards death—a choice of the closed world of systematic security substitutes, whether of a psychological or of a dogmatic kind. They bear witness to our refusal of the risk, of the risk of existence into which we are called (not "thrown," as in Heidegger). It is this refusal which makes us "opposite" to all things:

> "Who's turned us round like this, so that we always,
>   do what we may, retain the attitude
>   of someone who's departing? . . .
>   . . . .
>   we live our lives, forever taking leave."
>   (*Elegies,* VIII)

This persistent "farewell" of things is our perpetual running into emptiness, the always being opposite that makes us long to "fling the emptiness out of (our) arms." Instead of looking out from reality and up into the openness of our creative ascent,

> ". . . our eyes, as though reversed
>   encircle it on every side, like traps"

set round about to narrow and confine it—to conform it to our own refusal and to our own projections:

> ". . . for while a child's quite small we take it
>   and turn it round and force it to look backwards
>   at conformation. . . ."

The result is "we see only death." Even the animal, which has not developed our ego-consciousness, has an advantage here: for it has not learned "death," but

> "has its decease perpetually behind it
> and God in front, and when it moves, it moves
> into eternity, like running springs." . . .
> *(Elegies,* VIII)

So we should move, as on running springs, into eternity:
not, however, as animals, unconsciously one with the
life-urge, but precisely as men—whose distinguishing
mark it is that we transcend the world and its fatal momentums, and are called to the translation of all that is
mute into the higher significances of the infinite relatedness of things. It is to this vocation that we must bear
witness: when we refuse life's imperative we commit
ourselves to doctrines and configurations of descent and
death.

One of Rilke's early poems illuminates this:

> "You, neighbor God, if sometimes in the night
> I rouse you with loud knocking, I do so
> only because I seldom hear you breathe;
> I know: you are alone.
> And should you need a drink, no one is there
> to reach it to you, groping in the dark,
> Always I hearken. Give but a small sign.
> I am quite near.

> "Between us there is but a narrow wall,
> and by sheer chance; for it would take
> merely a call from your lips or from mine
> to break it down,
> and that without a sound.

> "The wall is builded of your images.

> "They stand before you hiding you like names,
> And when the light within me blazes high
> that in my inmost soul I know you by,
> the radiance is quandered on their frames.

> "And then my senses, which too soon grow lame,
> exiled from you, must go their homeless ways." [29]

The fine pathos of this poem is achieved through the poet's placing God, adroitly, in the position of a child, sleeping in a room above his parents. The child awakes and in the darkness feels solitary and alone, so he coughs or knocks a book from the shelf in the darkness, hoping to arouse the parent below. The good parent hears, of course, and coughs in return, or fetches the child a drink of water. The child is reassured. He is not alone. He relaxes and is soon asleep again. In this skillful inversion of the God-man relation, the loneliness of God shut off from men is movingly depicted. Actually it is the loneliness of man that is raised to the infinite.

But the irony falls at another point. That which shuts God out from communication with us is the ceiling of names which we have contrived for him. Our names for God ascend only so high. There they cluster, harden, are systematized and justified, and are finally substituted for God himself. Not only is God closed out, but we ourselves are trapped beneath the narrowing "objectivity" ("what Berdyaev would call our objectivization") of our image projections. We are left, under "God," to go our homeless ways. The very names of God exclude him, or leave us holding, in the name of God and in his absence, the husks of a former witness. It is here that Rilke, like Hölderlin before him, takes on himself the poetic-prophetic venture:

> "O you God that has vanished!
>   You infinite track
>   only because dismembering hatred dispersed you
>   are we hearers today and a mouth which else
>   nature would lack."
>
> (Sonnets, I, 26)

But it is not merely that Rilke holds to the "God beyond God" (Tillich) whereby we recognize that God is infinitely beyond our formulae for invoking or defining him. The real clue to Rilke's vision lies at another point:

"Who knows, I wonder (he wrote in one of his letters), whether we do not take the gods the wrong way about? (Perhaps it is only by ourselves that we are separated from their august and glorious countenance.) Who knows whether we are not very near to seeing the expression that we aspire to contemplate, only we are at the back?—and is not the only explanation this—that our faces and the divine eyes are turned in the same direction and only make one? How under these conditions could we come towards him from the depths of the space which is before him?" [30]

Religion, that is, is "a direction of the heart"; and we are not supposed to be looking *at* God. Our task is to see things as He sees them: to be looking in the same direction that He is looking.

The Old Testament he found to be "full of hands pointing." In the Koran he found "another mighty pointing hand." Then he comments:

"Christ doubtless wished to do the same. To point. But men here have been like dogs who do not understand pointing fingers but think they must snap at the hand. Instead of going onwards from the road of the Cross where the signpost had been erected high into the night of sacrifice, Christianity has settled there, declaring itself to live there in Christ. . . . And therefore they do not dwell in Christ." . . . [31]

From this it should be clear that the reason why Rilke never took the last step into Christianity was that within his spiritual vision there could be "no objective encounter" (Marcel) with God; religion was a direction of the heart.

We must repeat now what we said at the beginning: that our interest is not in Rilke primarily, but in what the existentialists see in Rilke. In the translation of all things into inwardness (*Weltinnenraum*) Rilke runs the risk of Narcissism. In his category of "the open" he runs the risk, as we have noted elsewhere [32] of intensifying infinitely his longing for wholeness through turning his gaze into a typically Romantic longing for the infinite. In his notions of the Angel and the Orpheus descent he runs the risk of "naming the god" after his own need to name the god—that is, with a myth projection of his quest. Holthusen has put this splendidly: "His personal myth is as it were a Franciscan and seraphic variation on Nietzsche's philosophy of Life and immanence." [33] Again and again one feels his poetic vision to be enervated by an ontological and moral deficiency, an estheticism, a flight from the crucial ontological decisiveness of the moment in time. He seems to effect here a golden volatilization of my response to reality dissolving the perpetual event of Otherness into the notional projection of "the Whole." The point is, however, that for Heidegger and for Marcel he means more than this. He performs for these philosophers an incarnational service. He embodies for Heidegger the "readiness for dread." With his lyre in his hands, he lets himself go into Nothing— frees himself, that is, "from the idols we all have"— and descends into the threat of annihilation which hides behind our temporal fixations; here he discovers "the all-but untrodden region of Being" from whence "everything that 'is' returns into *what* it is and is able to be" (from *What is Metaphysics*). For Marcel, he embodies fidelity to his calling, and his calling bears witness to the sustaining and informing Presence. Rilke stands between, so to speak, the two metaphysicians: he supplies the formal ideas of the one with a mythology and confirmation which translates it from the abstract forms

of Being into the concrete quests for God; he supplies
the other with an attestation of a reality "which at once
penetrates and enfolds him" (*Being and Having*, p. 211).
He became to the one a lyre on which Being and Nothing
might be played; to the other he was a willing and
obedient harp of Aeolus which sang respondingly to the
intermittent breathings of the Spirit.

But existentialism swings away here in separate directions. For all of Heidegger's brilliant reflective analysis,
one feels left in the regions of dearth, with nothing but
the absence of God to guarantee the movements from
what is to Nothingness to Being to the renewing of that
which is: that is to say, with Being falling away into
Nothing. In Marcel the movement is toward Presence. In
Heidegger we resume the classical problem (of Being)
with its Parmenidean oversight of existence—despite his
aim, by the enquiry into Nothing, to put us, the en-
quirers, ourselves in question. In Marcel we move to
concrete metaphysics: "surely it is of the essence of
anything ontological that it can be no more than at-
tested?" (*Being and Having*, p. 99.) In Heidegger we
move through "essential dread" to the experience of
awe—which clears and enfolds that region of human
being within which man endures, as at home, in the enduring ("Courage can endure Nothing"). But in Marcel
we move into *joy*. This is not *satisfaction*—which

"is something that happens within doors, in a *closed* creature;
but joy can only unfold beneath the open sky. It is radiant in its
very nature; it is like the sun at noonday. But we must not let the
spacial metaphor deceive us. The distinction between open and
closed only takes on its full meaning when we are speaking of
faith. Or, to go deeper still, when we are speaking of the free act
of the soul, as she wills or refuses to acknowledge that higher

principle which momentarily creates her and is the cause of her being, and as she makes herself penetrable or impenetrable to that transcendent yet inward action without which she is nothing."

(*Being and Having*, p. 216) [34]

Thus *awe* drops off into dread; *joy* springs up unto praise.

These distinctions enable us to understand why Romano Guardini holds that the essential thoughts of writers like Nietzsche, Hölderlin and Rilke are not to be understood out of their own centers, but only in their relation to Christian truth; and why he places Rilke within the tradition of those "philosophers of the heart" which runs from Augustine through Saint Francis and Dante to Pascal.[35]

Both Heidegger and Marcel begin, it is true, with man in the subjective immediacy of his own involvement, with his sense of "care" (cf. Tillich's "concern") and transcendence of himself in need—with man as a creature whose existence is at stake; nevertheless when Heidegger reaches his "open" I find myself mulling the refrain from *Tristan und Isolde* inserted by Eliot in his *Waste Land*—*Oed' und leer das Meer* (Vast and empty the sea . . .), whereas when we reach the "open" of Marcel it is a very easy step indeed to Dante's *In la sua voluntade est nostra pace,* provided we accept that will in watchfulness and trust. Or, to paraphrase a figure from the late Paul Elmer More, it is as if Heidegger were building himself a stately staircase at the crossing of roads and by it were mounting dialectically up—to nothing. Whereas the unacknowledged Christian power which informs the witness of Rilke as well as that of Marcel is of another kind: at the crossing of all the roads of human refusal and evasion there stands no ladder at all—but a Cross!

Now it is interesting to note that the moment the Cross is mentioned, it throws a precipitating and cathartic light on the whole problem of the naming of the gods. It shocks us out of the esthetic and out of the mystical—revealing those as temptations of the spirit to which both poet and philosopher quite easily succumb. The service-able mythology of Orpheus falls away like a curtain before the historicity of Christ. It (the Cross) draws upon itself all the existential contradictions of self and life and destiny and reveals them in their absolute im-plication. It even precipitates the godly immanence, becoming in time the God manifest. It breaks thereby my pretentions, restoring me to creaturehood, and re-storing my Original Option—the acceptance or refusal of love. The Cross existentializes my self in its flight from the God-relation; it existentializes our history from the intricate patterns of its will to be opposite (its com-pounded death-wish).

But what becomes, then, of the existentialist chal-lenge? What becomes of the death of God? and the es-sential return into the proximity of the Source? Do we not accept these claims? Must we not learn once more to be at home *at home*—re-cognizing the god? The answer is that indeed we do, but we hold that the authentic origin of these insights into the critique of Christendom arises, though as yet unre-cognized, from the Cross. As "Chris-tian" we must learn once more to be Christians—re-cog-nizing the Christ.

It is true, as Marcel holds, that the secret of a pious reverence for souls and *things* must be rediscovered today. It is true also that the Christian has been "tempted to over-accentuate the misery and degradation of the world left to itself, the better to emphasize the redemp-tive value of the supernatural forces which work upon

it both from above and from the depths of the soul"—
and that we risk sacrilege and the progressive unhallow-
ing of the world by so doing. More important still,
Christianity was taken captive by the objective systems,
and Christ himself was trapped in the substantialist
world-view. Christology *had* to be spoken in the two-
nature hypothesis because the Hellenic metaphysic
which the early Church adopted as its mold for meaning
required it; and the heresies of Docetism, Arianism, et
cetera, *had* to follow since the person of the Gospels was
other than the names which were hiding him. Sinners
had to be bound causally by "Adam's sin" since the
Aristotelian logic required it; but the heresies of man's
capacity and incapacity *had* to come since neither life
nor the Spirit could tolerate an existential tyranny of
extremes. Likewise our psychology, our cosmology, our
anthropology have changed, and are bringing us nearer
to the existentialism of the Scriptures. We begin to see
what the Old Testament saw: that

"Man is capable of despair, capable of hugging death, of hugging
his *own* death. A central datum for metaphysic, but such definitions of man as that proposed by Thomism cover it up and disguise
it. The essential merit of Kierkegaard and his school, to my mind,
is their having brought this datum into full view. And metaphysic
ought to take up its position just there, face to face with despair."
(Marcel: *Being and Having*, p. 104)

We are thus bent back upon ourselves; but upon
ourselves at the point of fidelity and integrity under God,
and upon ourselves within time and towards destiny. Our
problem, existentially, is not now the classical problem
of the One and the Many, but that of the *fullness* and
emptiness of time. It is not that "nothing stays for us"
(Pascal) or that "we live our lives, forever taking leave"
(Rilke); it is that my existence is an existence towards

death or an existence towards love. But this moves me
into history, not out of it. It discloses *within* history the
momentums of life and the momentums of death. Christ
occurs, existentially, where these two momentums collide
absolutely; and where the collision is absolute Christ's
action *recapitulates* the whole (from beginning to end),
as Irenaeus held, and his "victory" makes "eventual" the
New Being in the world.

Henceforth is clarified the two ages, the age of death
which is passing away, and the new aeon of the Promises
which are "running to meet us"! Not farewell, but greet-
ing! The children of Abraham according to the flesh
stand over against the children according to the promise.
Righteousness based on past performance and the legal
merit acquired thereby gives place to righteousness
based on the constantly proffered new gift of God. Our
ancient refusal of the gifts, which makes for emptiness
through severance of the relation, stands over against the
open election which, bringing fullness, penetrates and
reverses the momentums of death and in which the
Kingdom, though present, is running to meet us.

"Many Christians assume (writes Paul Minear) that Christology
consists primarily of an effort to define the relation of the second
member of the Trinity to the other members. This denies Jesus'
acceptance of his followers as his brothers. It obscures the New
Testament accent upon the *meeting of two human natures* in Jesus,
and its accent upon the way in which the New Man includes the
whole of the new age." [36]

The shifting of the Christological axis here not only
releases one from an entire metaphysical consciousness
within which the "Person and the Work of Christ" was
formulated, "hiding Him like names"; but the mytholo-
gies which were attached to it as its mediating means of
elucidation fall away also, making possible the recovery

of the historical-prophetic dimension. But the lesson of Hölderlin and Rilke is that it must be recovered in inwardness and patience, not in defiance and storm (Nietzsche). "Readiness for dread," says Heidegger, "is to say 'Yes!' to the inwardness of things, to fulfill the highest demand which alone touches man to the quick" (in *What Is Metaphysics*). "To live, for man," writes Marcel, "is to accept life, to say 'Yes' to life; or else the opposite, to vow himself to a state of internal war, when in appearance he is acting as if he is accepting something, which, deep down, he refuses . . ." (*Being and Having*, p. 95). Nietzsche too sought the "everlasting Yea!" The Apostle Paul found it, in what Minear calls "one of Paul's most profound, if little explored, Christological confessions": [37]

"In Him it is always Yes. For all the promises of God find their *Yes* in Him. That is why we utter *the Amen* through Him to the glory of God. But it is God who establishes you in Christ, and has commissioned us; he has put his seal upon us and given us His Spirit in our hearts as a guarantee." (II Cor. 1:19–22)

Rilke caught a glimpse of this, when, in the tenth *Elegy*, after climbing the Mountains of Primal Pain (his nearest approach, perhaps, to the night of Gethsemane), he glimpsed the depth of the simplicity of grace—as simple, perhaps, as rain that falls. If only the dead could tell us, could speak to us, he muses—

"look, they'd be pointing, perhaps, to the catkins, hanging
    from empty hazels, or else they'd be meaning the rain
    that falls on the dark earth in the early Spring.

"And we, who have always thought
    of happiness climbing, would feel
    the emotion that almost startles
    when happiness falls."

We strive so hard for "happiness"; instead of learning, quite simply, that grace burgeons from within like the catkins, or falls, in abundance, like the rain.

Nevertheless, both Hölderlin and Rilke must remain "forerunners" merely of the definition of need in our time of dearth. They seek a return to the Source without perceiving that the godly immanence as we must come to know it (that is, within history) is evocative of the Cross. Their Christ-figures—Empedocles, Orpheus— still force the kingdom. Empedocles learned that "to be alone and without gods, is death"; Orpheus sought to "be ever dead in Eurydice" (St. Paul's death in Christ) so to "mount more praisingly back into the pure relation." He learned that

> "The god is the place that is healing,
> Ever torn open anew by yourselves. . . ."
> (*Sonnets*, II, 13, 16)

By divinizing the poet, they would by-pass the cross, and so *mount* purely into the pure relation. They have not learned the existential ubiquity (and thereby the Christological seriousness) of Jesus' saying: "I am the way, the truth, and the life." Just as the philosopher of Being runs the risk of ceasing to be a man (through deleting himself from the problem), so the esthete runs the risk (as Rilke confessed) of by-passing the human. So he did not learn compassion. Rilke died from a thorn-prick received while gathering roses; Christ died from a spearthrust which gathers the wounds of the world.

FOOTNOTES

1. What Is Existentialism?

1. *The Logic of Hegel*, translated from *The Encyclopaedia of the Philosophical Sciences* by William Wallace. Second revised edition, Oxford University Press, 1892, p. 8.

2. *Universitas*, Heft 9, Jahrgang 7, 1952, article entitled "Martin Heidegger und die Sprache der Philosophen," p. 899.

3. *Theologische Studien*, Heft 34, 1952, p. 45.

4. From "To the Unknown God," translated by Walter A. Kaufmann in his *Nietzsche*, Princeton University Press, 1950, p. 371.

2. Sören Kierkegaard

1. Kierkegaard, Sören, *The Point of View*, translated by Walter Lowrie, Oxford University Press, 1939, pp. 5 and 6.

2. *Ibid.*, p. 6.

3. Miguel de Unamuno

1. October 26, 1953.

2. *Cf. Perplexities and Paradoxes*, translated by Stuart Gross, Philosophical Library, 1945, p. 51.

3. "En Torno al Casticismo," from *Publicaciones de la Residencia de Estudiantes*, 1916.

4. From "Vivo sin vivir en mi." *Cf.* translation by E. Allison Peers in *The Complete Works of Saint Teresa of Jesus*, Volume III, Sheed and Ward, 1950, p. 277.

5. *Cf.* "The Spanish Christ" in *Perplexities and Paradoxes*, pp. 75 ff.

6. *The Christ of Velazquez*, translated by Eleanor L. Turnbull, Johns Hopkins Press, 1951, pp. 7, 8.

7. *Ibid.*, p. 20.

8. *The Tragic Sense of Life*, translated by J. E. C. Flitch, Macmillan Co., 1921, pp. 263, 268 and 269.

9. *Poems by Miguel de Unamuno*, translated by Eleanor L. Turnbull, Johns Hopkins Press, 1952, p. 163.

10. *Perplexities and Paradoxes*, p. 2.

11. *Cf. The Tragic Sense of Life*, pp. 263 and 269.

12. *Cf. ibid.*, pp. 194, 195.

4. Nicholas Berdyaev

1. *Truth and Revelation*, Harper and Bros., 1953, p. 11. (Paris: YMCA-Press)
2. *Smysl Tvorchestva*, Moscow, 1916; English translation, *The Meaning of the Creative Act*, Harper and Bros., 1955.
3. *Truth and Revelation*, p. 12.
4. Berdyaev, Nicholas, *The Beginning and the End*, Geoffrey Bles, 1952, pp. 102–103.
5. *Ibid.*, pp. 135–136.
6. Berdyaev, Nicholas, *Slavery and Freedom*, Charles Scribner's Sons, 1944, pp. 48, 45 respectively.
7. *Theologia Germanica*, New York, 1949, p. 117.
8. *Truth and Revelation*, pp. 13–14.
9. *Slavery and Freedom*, pp. 82, 83.
10. *Ibid.*, p. 82; *cf. The Beginning and the End*, p. 151.
11. *Slavery and Freedom*, pp. 85, 89.
12. *Ibid.*, p. 172.
13. *The Divine Comedy*, translated by Dorothy L. Sayers, I: Hell, Canto III, Penguin Books.
14. *The Beginning and the End*, p. 227.
15. *The Divine and the Human*, Geoffrey Bles, 1949, p. 197.
16. *Ibid.*, p. 200.

5. Gabriel Marcel

1. *Being and Having*, Dacre Press, 1949, p. 15.
2. *Ibid.*, p. 20.
3. *Man against Mass Society*, Henry Regnery Co., 1952, p. 1.
4. *Homo Viator*, Henry Regnery Co., 1951, p. 134.

6. Martin Heidegger

1. *Holzwege*, Frankfurt, 1950, front page.
2. *Ibid.*, p. 294.
3. *Einführung in die Metaphysik*, Tübingen, 1953, pp. 281 f.
4. *Ibid.*, pp. 32, 34, and 35, respectively.

5. *Ibid.*, p. 65.

6. *Platon's Lehre von der Wahrheit* . . . , Bern, 1947, p. 92.

7. Quoted by Brand Blanshard, "Philosophical Style," in *The Yale Review*, 1953, p. 547.

8. For the English terminology compare Karl Löwith, "Heidegger: Problem and Background of Existentialism" in *Social Research*, Volume 15, 1948, pp. 348 ff. *Cf. Sein und Zeit*, Halle, 1927, pp. 5 ff. and 11 ff.

9. *Sein und Zeit*, pp. 336 ff.

10. *Ibid.*, pp. 27 ff.

11. *Ibid.*, pp. 63 ff. and 148 ff.

12. *Cf.* Karl Löwith *op. cit.*, p. 353.

13. *Sein und Zeit*, pp. 235 ff.

14. *Ibid.*, pp. 256 and 251.

15. *Ibid.*, pp. 140 and 186 ff.

16. *Ibid.*, p. 187.

17. *Ibid.*, p. 266.

18. *Cf.* Karl Löwith, *op. cit.*, p. 354.

19. *Cf. Einführung* . . . , p. 64.

20. *Cf. Holzwege*, p. 279.

21. See *Sein und Zeit*, pp. 397 ff. *Cf.* Karl Löwith, *Heidegger, Denker in Dürftiger Zeit*, Frankfurt, 1953, pp. 45 ff., and the excellent article by H. Ott, in *Theologische Rundschau*, 1953, pp. 63 ff.

22. *Cf.* for the term "historicity," E. Frank, *Philosophical Understanding and Religious Truth*, Oxford University Press, 1945, p. 133, note 1.

23. *Sein und Zeit*, pp. 372 ff., 326, and 329, respectively. See also H. Knittermeyer, *Die Philosophie der Existenz*, 1952, pp. 263 ff.

24. *Einführung* . . . , pp. 33 ff.

25. See *Über den Humanismus*, 1949, p. 17. *Cf.* Karl Löwith, *Heidegger, Denker* . . . , pp. 7–42.

26. See *Einführung* . . . , p. 84.

27. *Cf. Über den Humanismus*, p. 5.

28. *Cf. Holzwege*, p. 301 ff.

29. *Ibid.*, and also *Einführung* . . . , pp. 46 ff., and *Was ist Metaphysik*, 6th edition, p. 16.

30. *Cf. Holzwege*, pp. 319, 321.

31. *Ibid.*, pp. 310 ff.

32. *Ibid.*, pp. 300 ff.

33. *Holzwege*, p. 321.

34. *Ibid.*, p. 248.

35. *Ibid.*, p. 343.

36. Karl Jaspers' *Des Philosophische Glaube*, translated and published under the title, *The Perennial Scope of Philosophy*, Yale University Press, 1952.

37. Between 1926 and 1936 Martin Heidegger was co-editor of *Theologische Rundschau* along with H. von Soden and R. Bultmann. Bultmann dedicated Volume I of his *Glauben und Verstehen* to Heidegger.

38. *Holzwege*, p. 235.

39. *Platon's Lehre von der Wahrheit mit einem Brief über den Humanismus*, 1947, p. 112.

40. *Einführung* . . . , p. 5.

41. *Ibid.*, p. 34.

42. *Holzwege*, p. 234.

43. *Ibid.*, p. 70.

44. *Ibid.*, pp. 291 ff.

45. *Ibid.*, p. 303.

46. *Ibid.*, pp. 246, 247. *Cf. Einführung* . . . , p. 33.

8. On the Naming of the Gods in Hölderlin and Rilke

1. Sören Kierkegaard, "Diapsalmata" in *Either/Or*, translated by W. Lowrie, *et al.*, Princeton University Press, 1944, Volume I, p. 15.

2. *The New York Times Book Review*, July 19, 1953, p. 6.

3. Quoted in Marcel, *Homo Viator*, translated by Emma Crauford, Henry Regnery Co., 1951, p. 214.

4. *Ibid.*, p. 213

5. "Remembrance of the Poet" in *Existence and Being* (Introduction by Werner Brock), Vision Press, 1949, p. 285.

6. Gustav Thibon in *L'Existentialisme*, Librairie P. Téqui, 1947, p. 160.

7. *Cf.* Jacques Maritain, *The Degrees of Knowledge*, Scribners, 1938, pp. 359 ff.; also *Reflexions sur l'Intelligence*, Nouvelle Librairie Nationale, 1926, pp. 142, 150, and *De Bergson à Thomas d'Aquin*, Éditions de la Maison Française, Inc., 1944, p. 95; Erich Przywara, *Das Geheimnis Kierkegaards*, Verlag von R. Oldenbourg, 1929, pp. 9, 14, 123, 174.

8. *Pensées* (Brunschvig edition), Librairie Garnier Frères, 1925, #552, p. 216.

9. *Confessions*, X, xxvii, 38, translated by J. G. Pilkington, Liveright, 1927, pp. 247–248.

10. *Du Refus à l'Invocation*, pp. 109–110. Quoted by Thibon, *op. cit.*, p. 160.

11. *Ibid.*

12. "Hölderlin and the Essence of Poetry" in *Existence and Being*, p. 312.

13. *Ibid.*

14. *Cf.* Otto Friedrich Bollnow, *Rilke*, W. Kohlhammer Verlag, 1951, pp. 20–24.

15. *The Dedicated Life and Rainer Maria Rilke*, Burning Glass Paper No. 19, Ridgeway House, n. d., p. 11.

16. *Homo Viator*, p. 213.

17. *Holzwege*, Vittorio Klostermann, 1950, p. 283.

18. *Ibid.*, p. 273.

19. Quoted by Marcel in *Homo Viator*, p. 231.

20. *Letters to a Young Poet*, translated by M. D. Herter Norton, W. W. Norton and Co., 1934, pp. 69–70.

21. *Ibid.*, pp. 33–34.

22. *Ibid.*

23. W. B. Yeats, "Two Songs from a Play," II, in *Collected Poems*, Macmillan Co., 1935, p. 246.

24. Rilke, *Selected Letters*, translated by R. F. C. Hall, Macmillan & Co., Ltd. p. 385. Quoted in Marcel, *Homo Viator*, pp. 262–267, and Heidegger, *Holzwege*, p. 283.

25. *Selected Letters*, pp. 287–288. Quoted in Marcel, *Homo Viator*, p. 263.

26. Marcel, *ibid.*, p. 264.

27. *Liebe und Tod, Versuch einer Deutung und Auseinandersetzung mit Rainer Maria Rilke*, Verlag Herder, 1948, pp. 163–169.

28. *Selected Letters*, p. 335. Quoted in Marcel, *op. cit.*, p. 222.

29. *Poems from the Book of Hours*, translated by Babette Deutsch, New Directions, 1941, p. 13.

30. Quoted in Marcel, *op. cit.*, p. 240.

31. Quoted in F. W. Van Herrikhuizen, *Rainer Maria Rilke, His Life and Work*, translated by Fernand G. Renier and Anne Cliff, Philosophical Library, 1952, p. 357.

32. *Cf. Spiritual Problems in Contemporary Literature*, edited by Stanley Romaine Hopper, Harpers, 1952, p. 167.

33. Hans Egon Holthusen, *Rainer Maria Rilke, A Study of his Later Poetry*, translated by J. P. Stern, Yale University Press, 1952, p. 44.

34. *Being and Having*, A. and C. Black, Ltd., 1949.

35. *Zu Rainer Maria Rilkes Deutung des Daseins*, Verlag A. Francke Ag., 1946, pp. 59, 117n.

36. "The Time of Hope in the New Testament" in *The Scottish Journal of Theology*, Volume 6, No. 4, December 1953, p. 353.

37. *Ibid.*, p. 355 (note change in wording).

The quotations on pages 164–165 from Hölderlin's hymn *Patmos* and on page 168 from *The Journey* are taken from *Poems*, translated by Michael Hamburger, published in New York by Pantheon Books, 1953, and here used by permission.

The various quotations from Rilke's Sonnets are taken from Rainer Maria Rilke, *Sonnets to Orpheus*, translated by J. B. Leishman, published in London by the Hogarth Press, 1946, and here used by permission.

The various quotations from Rilke's Elegies are taken from Rainer Maria Rilke, *Duino Elegies*, Translation, Introduction and Commentary by J. B. Leishman and Stephen Spender, published in New York by W. W. Norton and Company, 1939, and here used by permission.

BIBLIOGRAPHY

The following is a selected list of works by and about the existentialists. Only works not repeatedly cited in the text of this volume are included. For the most part the books listed are not prohibitively technical. Most are currently in print in English, and a few can be obtained in reasonably priced paper-bound editions. The list is intended for the guidance of the reader who wishes to take another step toward an understanding of the existentialists.

1. What Is Existentialism?

James Collins, *The Existentialists.* Chicago, Henry Regnery Co., 1952.

Karl Jaspers, *Way to Wisdom: An Introduction to Philosophy.* Tr. Ralph Manheim. New Haven, Yale University Press, 1951.

Helmut Kuhn, *Encounter with Nothingness: An Essay on Existentialism.* Chicago, Henry Regnery Co., 1949.

Emmanuel Mounier, *Existentialist Philosophies.* Tr. Eric Blow. London, Rockliff, 1948.

Jean-Paul Sartre, *Existentialism.* Tr. Bernard Frechtman. New York, Philosophical Library, 1947.

Paul Tillich, "Existential Philosophy" in *The Journal of the History of Ideas,* Vol. 5, Jan., 1944, pp. 44–70.

2. Sören Kierkegaard

The Journals of Sören Kierkegaard. Tr. Alexander Dru. London, Oxford University Press, 1938.

A Kierkegaard Anthology. Edited by Robert Bretall. Princeton, Princeton University Press, 1947.

Philosophical Fragments. Tr. David F. Swenson. Princeton, Princeton University Press, 1936.

Sickness unto Death and *Fear and Trembling.* Tr. Walter Lowrie. Paper-bound edition, New York, Doubleday Anchor Books, 1954.

Walter Lowrie, *A Short Life of Kierkegaard.* London, Oxford University Press, 1942.

David F. Swenson, *Something about Kierkegaard.* Minneapolis, Augsburg Publishing House, 1945.

3. *Miguel de Unamuno*

The Tragic Sense of Life. New York, Dover Publications, Inc., paper-bound edition, 1954.

The Agony of Christianity. Tr. Pierre Loving. New York, 1928.

The Life of Don Quixote and Sancho. Tr. H. P. Earle. New York, Alfred A. Knopf, Inc., 1927.

Three Exemplary Novels. Evergreen Books.

4. *Nicholas Berdyaev*

Dream and Reality. An Autobiography. Tr. Katharine Lampert. New York, Macmillan Co., 1950.

Freedom and the Spirit. Tr. O. F. Clarke. London, G. Bles, Ltd., 1935.

The Meaning of History. Tr. George Reavey. London, G. Bles, Ltd., 1936.

The Destiny of Man. Tr. Natalie Duddington. London, G. Bles, Ltd., 1937.

Solitude and Society. Tr. George Reavey. London, G. Bles, Ltd., 1938.

Matthew Spinka, *Nicholas Berdyaev, Captive of Freedom.* Philadelphia, Westminster Press, 1950.

5. *Gabriel Marcel*

Metaphysical Journal. Tr. Bernard Wall. Chicago, Henry Regnery Co., 1952.

Being and Having. Tr. Katharine Farrer. London, Dacre Press, 1949. Especially Pt. I, Ch. I, "A Metaphysical Diary."

The Philosophy of Existence. Tr. Manya Harari. Philosophical Library, 1949. Especially pp. 77 ff, "An Essay in Autobiography."

Homo Viator. Introduction to a Metaphysic of Hope. Tr. Emma Crauford. Chicago, Henry Regnery Co., 1951.

The Mystery of Being. 2 volumes. (The Gifford Lectures), Chicago, Henry Regnery Co., 1950 and 1951.

6. Martin Heidegger

Existence and Being, Introduction by Werner Brock. An Account of *Sein und Zeit* with a translation of several philosophical essays. Chicago, Henry Regnery Co., 1949.

Martin Buber, "The Doctrine of Heidegger," pp. 163–181 in *Between Man and Man*. Tr. Ronald Gregor Smith. New York, Macmillan Co., 1948.

Erich Dinkler, "Existentialist Interpretation of the New Testament," *The Journal of Religion*, April, 1952, pp. 87 ff.

F. H. Heinemann, *Existentialism and the Modern Predicament*. New York, Harper and Bros., 1953. Chapter VI, "Heroic Defiance" (unsympathetic but instructive).

John Macquarrie, *An Existentialist Theology*, A comparison of Heidegger and Bultmann. New York, Macmillan Co., 1955.

Michael Wyschogrod, *Kierkegaard and Heidegger*. London, Routledge & Kegan Paul, 1954 (technical discussion).

7. Existentialist Aspects of Modern Art

Otto Benesch, *Art of the Northern Renaissance*. Cambridge, 1947. Chapter entitled "Extremists in Art and Religion," being mainly a discussion of Grünewald's Isenheim altarpiece.

Nicholas Berdyaev, *The Meaning of the Creative Act*. New York, Harper and Bros., 1955. Chapter X, "Art and Theurgy."

Albert Camus, *The Rebel*. New York, Alfred A. Knopf, 1954. Chapter IV, "Revolt and Art."

Masters of Modern Art. Edited by Alfred H. Barr, Jr. New York, The Museum of Modern Art, 1954. Deluxe reproductions of the art housed in New York City's Museum of Modern Art, with interpretations.

Edgar Wind, "Traditional Religion and Modern Art" in *Art News*, May, 1953.

8. On the Naming of the Gods in Hölderlin and Rilke

Martin Heidegger, *Existence and Being*, London, Vision Press, 1949, pp. 251–315. On Hölderlin.

Gabriel Marcel, *Homo Viator*, tr. by Emma Crauford, Chicago, Henry Regnery Co., 1951, pp. 213–270. On Rilke.

Albert Camus, *The Rebel*, New York, Alfred A. Knopf, 1954. Chapter II, "The Revolt of Poetry."

Hölderlin, His Poems. Tr. Michael Hamburger. London, Havrill Press, 1942.

Rainer Maria Rilke, *Sonnets to Orpheus.* Tr. M. D. Herter Norton. New York, W. W. Norton & Co., Inc., 1942.

Rainer Maria Rilke, *Duino Elegies.* Translation, Introduction and Commentary by J. B. Leishman and Stephen Spender. New York, W. W. Norton & Co., Inc., 1939.

L. S. Salzberger, *Hölderlin, A Study of His Life, Vision and Poetry.* New Haven, Yale University Press, 1952.

Hans Egon Holthusen, *Rainer Maria Rilke, A Study of His Later Poetry.* Tr. by J. P. Stern. New Haven, Yale University Press, 1952.

INDEX